26 Creative

Celebrations for All Generations

Interactive Prayers, Gospel Reflections, and Activities for the Liturgical Year

SR. M. VALERIE SCHNEIDER, SND

TWENTY THIRD 23rd
PUBLICATIONS

Twenty-Third Publications
A Division of Bayard
One Montauk Avenue, Suite 200
New London, CT 06320
(860) 437-3012 or (800) 321-0411
www.23rdpublications.com

ISBN 978-1-58595-702-6
Library of Congress Catalog Card Number: 2008925302
Printed in the U.S.A.

Contents

Introduction

Intergenerational prayer and faith sharing are hardly a new development. In fact, they are as old as the New Testament. For example, while the Christian community was listening to Paul, a young lad named Eutychus fell asleep and fell from the third story (Acts 20:7–12). Some Scripture scholars claim that the apostle John was just a boy. If so, this youngster was honored with witnessing the Transfiguration and responsibility of taking care of Mary. A young lad with loaves and fish was the hero of the day in a large crowd of men, women, and children who were getting hungry after listening to Jesus' teaching. The teenage Mary visited her cousin Elizabeth who was having a baby in her old age, and they spent three months discussing the amazing kindness of God. Jesus himself in his pre-adolescent years listened to the religious teachers in the temple and asked them questions, amazing them with his intelligence. As an adult, Jesus enjoyed children and used the image of a child to symbolize the citizens of heaven. Jesus "miracled" and ministered with all ages.

The twenty-six units in this book, many based on the church year, are designed for Christian groups of mixed ages from small children to octogenarians. Groups experienced in faith sharing and those who are trying it for the first time will find the book user-friendly and enjoyable. Each unit includes something for everyone: questions appropriate to any age, creative actions to capture the short attention span of children, activities for families and mixed-age groups, and prayer that all can understand.

Each unit contains an opening prayer, a Scripture reading (usually from the gospels), a reflection with activity, discussion questions, suggestions for application, closing prayer, and additional activities for families or groups. The format allows for flexibility in length of time and selection of components. With limited discussion the unit could be accomplished within thirty minutes. Those with large blocks of time could utilize more of the activities and extend discussion.

If an intergenerational program is already in place, these units may provide creative additional ideas. Watch cheerleaders cheer the Risen Lord on Easter. Win a laughing contest on Mardi Gras. Join a line dance on All Saints Day. Enjoy an egg hunt at Easter and a cakewalk in Ordinary Time. (Many of the activities require some preparation and rehearsal to make the best impression; consequently, it will be wise for the leaders to look ahead to future weeks.)

In addition to intergenerational programs, the units can contribute to religious education programs, Vacation Bible School, Liturgy of the Word for Children, and parochial schools when only youth attend. These settings, too, have occasional opportunities for intergenerational gatherings, such as Grandparents Day.

What is spiritually enriching for one age group is potentially beneficial for other age groups. Youth appreciate the wisdom of older persons, and older persons grow younger when listening to the simplicity of little ones. After all, Christians are on the same journey; it is only the walking rate that differs.

All Saints and All Souls Days

BEFORE YOU BEGIN

Materials: (optional) photos of deceased relatives and pictures of canonized saints

To do: assign readers; place all children within a circle(s) of adults

SONG

Song appropriate to All Saints and All Souls Days or song of worship

OPENING PRAYER

Leader   Occasionally the Church prays a Litany of the Saints. At the Easter Vigil, at priestly ordinations, at baptisms, and at other times we call on the saints in heaven to bless us. Let us stand in a circle and take turns saying aloud the name of someone who has died or the name of a favorite saint. After each name, the group will respond "Pray for us."

READING: *Matthew 18:1–4*
(Place all the children in the center as the gospel account is read)

Narrator   The disciples came to Jesus and asked,

Disciples   Who is the greatest in the kingdom of heaven?

Narrator   Jesus called a child, whom he put among them, and said,

Jesus   Truly I tell you, unless you change and become like children, you will never enter the kingdom of heaven. Whoever becomes humble like this child is the greatest in the kingdom of heaven. Whoever welcomes one such child in my name welcomes me.

REFLECTION

Participants form a line, one behind the other, hands on the shoulders of the person ahead of them. Walk or dance to music. When the music stops, one or two drop off the end of the line. The music starts again, then stops, until only a few are left.

All people on earth are on a journey to heaven. We travel awhile together, but occasionally someone "drops out of line" through death. Think of all the persons who were on the journey with you but have died—parents, grandparents, friends, babies, parishioners, classmates. They are at their destination in heaven. We honor these persons today. We cheer for them, because they have won the race. They are the victors! We honor them as saints on All Saints and All Souls Days.

Sometimes we feel sad; we miss these persons who are now in heaven. Sometimes we feel guilty that we don't think of them very often. Sometimes we feel happy, because they are completely happy. Whatever we feel, these saints know how we feel, because their hearts can still touch ours. They live in God, so they are not bound by time and space the way we are. When our friends and relatives were on earth, they could not be with us all the time. Now they can. On earth we heard their voices; now they are soundless, but they participate in God who constantly tells us how much we are loved. So we can think of these saints as loving us with the very love of God. Stop for a few moments now and imagine hearing one of your loved ones telling you, "I love you." (*Pause a minute.*) Someday we will all be in heaven together. Let's pretend we're dancing in heaven. Let's form our line again, but this time no one drops out. And imagine all your loved ones being interspersed among you.

Everyone forms the line again to walk or dance. This time pretend everyone is in heaven, so no one drops out of line. This demonstrates that although the deceased are gone, they are still alive, and we will join them again.

SHARING

▶ Why do you think Jesus selected children as the model for sainthood?

▶ How do you picture heaven?

▶ A saint is someone with eternal life. Because our baptism gave us eternal life (grace), we are saints. How does your title "saint" make you feel?

▶ The fact that Jesus told the disciples that they had to "change" indicates that they needed a 180-degree turn in their thinking about the kingdom of God. What attitudes do you need to change to be ready for the kingdom of heaven?

▶ What do you understand by the "communion of saints" listed in the Creed?

ACTION STEP

Tell or write stories about the deceased to preserve their memory.

Attend an occasion that remembers the dead.

Clean up or decorate graves.

CLOSING PRAYER

Leader   All saints who have gone before us, be with us as we pray.

All   Hear us, all saints in heaven. Be our companions on the journey to heaven. Give us direction, remove obstacles, and keep our spirits strong. Help us make our decisions and actions like yours, as you followed Christ closely. Dear patron saints, be our model of love of God and neighbor. As we imitate you and pray to you, bless us and protect us.

OPTIONAL ACTIVITIES FOR FAMILIES OR GROUPS

1. Create a Litany of Saints from your family and friends. Pray it often, and continue to add names.

2. If children do not know their relatives well, together draw a diagram to understand relationships. Draw a halo, flower, or other symbol by those who have died.

3. Wear a saint's costume for Halloween, and tell "ghost stories" about the deaths of martyrs.

4. Remember that children learn prayer and virtue in the home, "the domestic Church." Include prayer with children or the entire family in your day.

God Is a Beautiful Word

– ADVENT –

BEFORE YOU BEGIN

Materials: (optional) Advent symbols, such as Advent wreath or Jesse tree, violet cloth

SONG

Song with Advent theme or reference to Jesus as the Word of God

OPENING PRAYER

Leader   God, our Master Craftsman, chisel from us whatever prevents us from being an image of you. Speak to us, and give us the ability to hear. We are open. May we receive from your fullness, grace upon grace. Let us now have silent prayer to listen to God speak to us. (*Three minutes of silent prayer*)

READING: *John 1:1–5, 14, 16–18*

In the beginning was the Word, and the Word was with God, and the Word was God. He was in the beginning with God. All things came into being through him, and without him not one thing came into being. What has come into being in him was life, and the life was the light of all people. The light shines in the darkness, and the darkness did not overcome it. And the Word became flesh and lived among us, and we have seen his glory, the glory as of a father's only son, full of grace and truth. From his fullness we have all received, grace upon grace. The law indeed was given through Moses; grace and truth came through Jesus Christ. No one has ever seen God. It is God the only Son, who is close to the Father's heart, who has made him known.

REFLECTION

As the leader reads the reflection, participants may "sign" the phrases "word upon word" and "grace upon grace" by putting one fist on top of the other, back and forth, as their arms go upward. Asterisks (*) indicate appropriate times.

Writing is hard work. Writers need to write word upon word.* Sometimes writers say they have "writer's block." They can't think of the words to type into the computer. They can't place word upon word.* But let's look at a different kind of writer's block. Did you ever see someone carve something beautiful from a block of wood? In a way, a writer is like that craftsman. A writer has something to share. The writer's thoughts are like a block of wood. Somehow a writer carefully chisels, and a story or poem appears—word upon word.*

Now let's think of God as a craftsman and a writer. From all eternity God the Craftsman worked, and the divine plan emerged like grace upon grace.* Creature by creature God saw that everything was very good. God made trees and tulips, snow and snapdragons, frogs and fruit, ponds and people—everything. Each created thing was like grace upon grace.* Then in the fullness of time God sent his Son, Jesus, like grace upon grace.* Jesus was called the Word, because he came from the Almighty Writer. Jesus was God the Writer's best Word. But Jesus wasn't created like all the other beings God created. No, for "In the beginning was the Word, and the Word was with God, and the Word was God" (Jn 1:1). Jesus was the Father's Masterpiece but equal to the Creative Father. This Word "became flesh and lived among us" (Jn 1:14). And the Creator continues to speak through his Word. We hear the Word, and "from his fullness we have all received grace upon grace"* (Jn 1:16).

SHARING

▶ There are many metaphors for Jesus, such as Good Shepherd, Way, Truth, Life, Bread of Life, Vine, Word, and many others. Which is your favorite metaphor for Jesus? Why?

▶ Can you imagine yourself being designed, crafted by God? How does that feel?

▶ Although December may be a busy month, Advent reminds us to take time to be quiet before God in prayer and waiting. How are you able to become quiet? How do you find time for God? How can the shopping, gift wrapping, and parties of December become part of your prayer?

ACTION STEP

Participants write their personal name for God on a tree ornament. Place these ornaments on a Christmas tree, and use this tree as an Advent decoration.

Buy Christmas gifts from organizations that help impoverished parts of the world.

Plan to spend extra time in prayer listening to Jesus, the Word of God.

Jesus is the Light of the Word shining in the darkness. When you see Christmas lights, think of Jesus the Light of the World, and ask him to replace war with peace.

CLOSING PRAYER

Leader	O Wisdom,
All	help us know how to live our discipleship.
Leader	O Sacred Lord,
All	help us make you more important than anything else.
Leader	O Root of Jesse,
All	help us honor the memory of those who have gone before us.
Leader	O Key of David,
All	unlock whatever prevents us from being close to you.
Leader	O Radiant Dawn,
All	shine upon our earth darkened by terror and violence.
Leader	O King of All Nations,
All	unite all nations, making us one world.
Leader	O Emmanuel, God-with-us,
All	help us feel your nearness this Christmas.

OPTIONAL ACTIVITIES FOR FAMILIES OR GROUPS

1. Write a poem that lets you emerge from your "writer's block." Try a haiku, a three-line poem whose first and third lines are five syllables and whose middle line is seven syllables. Write about an Advent theme, such as silence or waiting.

2. Make a poster of the metaphors for God in the Bible.

3. Instead of a gift exchange buy gifts for the needy.

4. Give the gift of service, such as cleaning a house, decorating a church, baking cookies for someone no longer able to do so.

Immaculate Conception

BEFORE YOU BEGIN

Materials: (optional) statue or picture of Mary, flowers, candles, maracas

To do: assign readers (and perhaps actors, if you wish the reading dramatized)

SONG

Song honoring Mary

OPENING PRAYER

Leader	Mary, we honor you under your title of Immaculate Conception.
All	Mary, full of grace, ask your Son to bless us.
Leader	Mary, we honor you, for from the first moment of your life you were full of grace and free from sin.
All	Mary, full of grace, ask your Son to bless us.
Leader	Mary, we honor you, for you were chosen before the beginning of the world to be completely holy.
All	Mary, full of grace, ask your Son to bless us.

Leader	Mary, we honor you, for you stayed away from sin your whole life.
All	Mary, full of grace, ask your Son to bless us.

READING: *Luke 1:26–38 (This reading could be pantomimed)*

Narrator 1	The angel Gabriel was sent by God to a town in Galilee called Nazareth, to a virgin engaged to a man whose name was Joseph, of the house of David. The virgin's name was Mary. And he came to her and said,
Gabriel	Greetings, favored one! The Lord is with you.
Narrator 2	But she was much perplexed by his words and pondered what sort of greeting this might be. The angel said to her,
Gabriel	Do not be afraid, Mary, for you have found favor with God. And now, you will conceive in your womb and bear a son, and you will name him Jesus. He will be great, and will be called the Son of the Most High, and the Lord God will give to him the throne of his ancestor David. He will reign over the house of Jacob forever, and of his kingdom there will be no end.
Narrator 1	Mary said to the angel,
Mary	How can this be, since I am a virgin?
Narrator 2	The angel said to her,
Gabriel	The Holy Spirit will come upon you, and the power of the Most High will overshadow you; therefore the child to be born will be holy; he will be called Son of God. And now, your relative Elizabeth in her old age has also conceived a son; and this is the sixth month for her who was said to be barren. For nothing will be impossible with God.
Narrator 1	Then Mary said,
Mary	Here am I, the servant of the Lord; let it be with me according to your word.
Narrator 2	Then the angel departed from her.

REFLECTION

> *At the asterisk, maracas help accompany the syncopated rhythm as participants speak the sentence "Nothing's impossible, nothing's impossible, nothing's impossible with God!"*

How do you feel when you're facing something impossible? Do you find yourself saying something like "It will take a miracle"? When the angel Gabriel asked Mary to be the mother of the Messiah, she did not understand how that would happen. However, the angel reminded her that…* Events in our lives may seem impossible. Getting your Christmas shopping finished may seem impossible, but…* Finishing projects for school and taking semester exams may seem impossible, but…* Coping with illness, taking care of the elderly, finding a better job, stopping an addiction, or losing weight may seem impossible, but….*

SHARING

▶ How does your faith help you when events seem impossible to you?

▶ How do you experience Mary as mother?

▶ How can you respond to those who object to Catholics' devotion to Mary?

▶ Mary was the first dwelling place of God on earth. Who and what are other "dwelling places" of God?

▶ The United States is under the patronage of Mary, the Immaculate Conception. How can Mary be a model for our country and our citizenship?

ACTION STEP

Pray to Mary for protection on the United States and good persons to lead the country.

CLOSING PRAYER

Leader   Please respond "Pray for us."
Mary, Immaculate Conception, (R)
Mary, First Disciple, (R)
Mary, Mother of the Redeemer, (R)
Mary, Hearer and Doer of the Word, (R)
Mary, Mother of All People, (R)
Mary, Mother of the Church, (R)
Mary, Model of bringing others to Christ, (R)
Mary, Queen of Apostles, (R)
Mary, Witness to the Gospel, (R)

OPTIONAL ACTIVITIES FOR FAMILIES AND GROUPS

1. Draw a stained glass window of Mary.

2. Pray for persons, groups, and churches who bear the name of Mary.

3. Pretend you are a TV or radio announcer at the time of Mary's birth. Announce on WNAZ, Nazareth's station, the birth of Mary to her parents Anne and Joachim.

4. Pretend you are Mary visiting her cousin Elizabeth. Tell Elizabeth about the Angel Gabriel.

5. View a segment of a movie dealing with the Annunciation.

Glory to God in the Highest Heaven!

- CHRISTMAS -

BEFORE YOU BEGIN

Materials: Spotlight, nativity scene, other Christmas decorations

To do: Assign readers and children to hold figures from nativity scene

SONG

Christmas carol, preferably "Angels We Have Heard on High"

OPENING PRAYER

Leader   With joy at the birth of Jesus, we pray.

All   Glory to the Father for giving us his Son! Honor to Mary for being willing to be the Mother of God! Honor to Saint Joseph for his courage and wisdom and care of the Holy Family! Honor to the angels who announced the birth of Jesus and continue their song of praise forever! Honor to all those who recognize Jesus as the savior! Saints and angels in heaven, join us in our praise.

READING: *Luke 2:4–18*

Narrator 1   Joseph went from the town of Nazareth in Galilee to Judea, to a city of David called

Bethlehem. He went to be registered with Mary, who was expecting a child. While they were there, the time came for her to deliver her child. And she gave birth to her firstborn son and wrapped him in bands of cloth, and laid him in a manger, because there was no place for them in the inn.

Narrator 2   In that region there were shepherds living in the fields, keeping watch over their flock by night. Then an angel of the Lord stood before them, and the glory of the Lord shone around them, and they were terrified. But the angel said to them,

Angel   Do not be afraid; for see—I am bringing you good news of great joy for all the people: to you is born this day in the city of David a Savior, who is the Messiah, the Lord. This will be a sign for you: you will find a child wrapped in bands of cloth and lying in a manger.

Narrator 3   And suddenly there was with the angel a multitude of the heavenly host, praising God and saying,

Angel   Glory to God in the highest heaven, and on earth peace among those whom he favors!

Narrator 4   When the angels had left them and gone into heaven, the shepherds said to one another,

Shepherd   Let us go now to Bethlehem and see this thing that has taken place, which the Lord has made known to us.

Narrator 5   So they went with haste and found Mary and Joseph, and the child lying in the manger. When they saw this, they made known what had been told them about this child; and all who heard it were amazed at what the shepherds told them.

REFLECTION

Participants hold figures from the nativity scene as they are spoken about.

We never tire hearing the Christmas story. We remember how **JOSEPH** had to be enrolled in the census in Bethlehem. **JOSEPH AND MARY** could not find a place in the inn, so they went to a stable where there were **ANIMALS.** On the hillsides there were **SHEPHERDS AND SHEEP**. At the time Jesus was born shepherds were looked down upon, because they could not observe all the rules of the Law of Moses. But God chose shepherds whose sheep would perhaps become food at Passover or be sacrificed in the Temple. When the baby Jesus grew up, the people would no longer need the celebration of Passover or the sacrifice of lambs in the Temple. Jesus himself became the Lamb of God, whose sacrifice on the cross was once and for all; no other animal sacrifices were needed. And Jesus would be the Temple; no temple made from stone would be needed. An **ANGEL** announced the good news of the birth of Jesus, and the whole sky was filled with **ANGELS** crying out, "Glory to God in the highest heaven, and on earth peace among those whom he favors!" (Lk 2:14). The shepherds went to see, and they, too praised God the way the angels did. Eventually the **WISE MEN** or **THREE KINGS** came to see the newborn king heralded by the **STAR**. Legend gives the three kings' names: Caspar, Melchior, and Balthasar. These wise men brought gold fit for a king, incense fit for a priest to offer sacrifice, and myrrh for anointing someone who was to die. We see that there is a lot of meaning tucked into the story of the birth of Jesus. We get clues about the end of the story when Jesus will become the king of the heavenly kingdom, the priest of the New Law, and the savior who will die and rise for us.

SHARING

▶ What is your favorite part of the Christmas story? Why?

▶ Why do you think God chose Mary and Joseph, shepherds and wise men?

ACTION STEP

The Christmas Season lasts until the Feast of the Baptism of Our Lord. Keep Christmas going after December 25 by keeping up decorations, postponing some parties until the Church's Christmas season, and saving a present or two until the Feast of Epiphany.

Jesus was born in a poor stable and first seen by poor shepherds. Remember those in poverty this Christmas through donations.

CLOSING PRAYER

Leader	Son of God and Son of Mary, you came to live among us.
All	Help us see you as you continue to live in the people around us.
Leader	Savior of the World, a star proclaimed your coming, and you yourself are the Light of the World.
All	May we be like Christmas lights to others who need comfort.
Leader	Jesus, Priest, King, and Perfect Sacrifice, you are the way to the kingdom.
All	Let the light of your star always guide us to you that we may be with you in heaven.

OPTIONAL ACTIVITIES FOR FAMILIES OR GROUPS

1. Arrange the figures in the nativity scene to reflect the characters in the gospels of Luke and Matthew.

2. Bless the Christmas decorations in and around your home. Ask God to remind you of himself, the best Christmas Gift, when you enjoy them.

3. Visit those who may be lonely after the busyness of Christmas subsides.

4. Research the feasts that occur between Christmas and the Baptism of Our Lord, such as St. Stephen, St. John, and Mary, the Mother of God.

Holy Family

BEFORE YOU BEGIN

Materials: photos of families, picture or statue of Holy Family, Christmas decoration, "prefabricated walls" with words needed in Reading

To do: assign readers and persons to "build a house"

SONG

Song about the Holy Family or a Christmas carol

OPENING PRAYER
(Children may hold photos of their families as the opening prayer is prayed)

Leader	O God, bless our families.
All	Give our family holiness.
Leader	When we are irritated or get on each other's nerves,
All	Give our family holiness.
Leader	When we quarrel and fight,
All	Give our family holiness.

Leader	When we say hurtful things,
All	Give our family holiness.
Leader	When we work together,
All	Give our family holiness.
Leader	When we play together,
All	Give our family holiness.
Leader	When we pray together,
All	Give our family holiness.

READING: *Colossians 3:12–15*

As the reading is read, participants may "build" a house of love by adding "prefabricated walls" made from poster board and labeled with the words in boldface print. You can make four walls with two words each, or "patience" and "love" can be doors, and "peace" can be half of the roof. The last piece is the roof labeled "thanksgiving."

Reader 1	As God's chosen ones, holy and beloved, clothe yourselves with **COMPASSION,** (*pause for part of the house to be placed*)
Reader 2	**KINDNESS,** (*pause*)
Reader 3	**HUMILITY,** (*pause*)
Reader 4	**MEEKNESS,** (*pause*)
Reader 5	and **PATIENCE.** (*pause*)
Reader 1	Bear with one another and, if anyone has a complaint against another, forgive each other; just as the Lord has forgiven you.
Reader 2	Above all, clothe yourselves with **LOVE.** (*pause*)
Reader 3	And let the **PEACE** of Christ rule in your hearts, to which indeed you were called in the one body. (*pause*)
Reader 4	And **BE THANKFUL.**

REFLECTION *(At the asterisk participants say "Holy, holy, holy.")*

Family life may seem ordinary—not the stuff for a big Church celebration like today's feast. But that is exactly what we are celebrating—the ordinary lives of Jesus, Mary, and Joseph in their home in Nazareth. Mary and Joseph taught Jesus to walk and talk.* Joseph showed Jesus how to pound a nail.* Jesus enjoyed watching his mother bake bread.* Jesus went to school and played with the neighborhood gang.* Joseph worked hard and charged an honest price for his carpentry.*

Our families become holy, too, by doing ordinary things well—the way Jesus, Mary, and Joseph would have done them. Parents work hard to pay the bills.* Children help in the house and yard.* Families go shopping, see movies, go on vacation, clean up the yard, plant gardens, watch TV, play games, and visit relatives.*

Praying and reading the Bible and doing good deeds can make us holy, but the best way to become holy like Jesus, Mary, and Joseph is simply to do what we are supposed to do and do it well.

SHARING

▶ Which virtue (part of the house) is most needed by your family?

▶ How does your family reflect Jesus Christ?

▶ Is it difficult to be holy?

▶ What is a burden to you in your household or family? Could this burden also be a blessing?

▶ What are the ordinary ways you can become holy?

ACTION STEP

Plan a special day for the family. Include prayer, play, and food.

Bring out photos or scrapbooks or a family tree. As you enjoy these items, include comments on the goodness (holiness) these persons have displayed.

Invite persons who may be lonely to a family party or outing.

Visit a family member whom you have not seen recently.

Study immigration laws to understand their role in the breakup of families.

CLOSING PRAYER

Leader	Let us pray that the peace of Christ reign in our hearts and homes. So that the world will become a place of peace,
All	Let peace be in our hearts and homes.
Leader	So that the world will become a place of forgiveness.
All	Let forgiveness be in our hearts and homes.
Leader	So that the world will become a place of happiness.
All	Let happiness be in our hearts and homes.
Leader	So that the world will become a place of joy,
All	Let joy be in our hearts and homes.
Leader	So that the world will become a place of love,
All	Let love be in our hearts and homes.

OPTIONAL ACTIVITIES FOR FAMILY OR GROUPS

1. On a thin piece of material write virtues that are important to the family, such as peace, joy, hope, forgiveness. Put the family surname in the middle of the material, and perhaps decorate or add a coat-of-arms. When finished, hang the banner in a place where it will move. Let the movement be like a prayer rising to God, asking God that these virtues will be part of the household.

2. Make a resolution to do something together every Sunday as a family.

3. If your family does not pray together, decide upon a time and place for family prayer.

Mardi Gras

BEFORE YOU BEGIN

Materials: (optional) cloth and beads in the colors of Mardi Gras, picture of Jesus laughing, eight signs for the Beatitudes

To do: Assign eight children to carry signs with words from the Beatitudes. Make halos or stars and signs with words from the Beatitudes.

SONG

Song about the Beatitudes or any lively or fun song

OPENING PRAYER

Leader	God of Laughter, you delighted in creation and saw it as good.
All	God of Laughter, give us joy.
Leader	God of Laughter, you delighted persons when you heard their prayer to do the impossible.
All	God of Laughter, give us joy.
Leader	God of Laughter, you triumphed over sin and sadness.
All	God of Laughter, give us joy.

Leader	God of Laughter, you hear our laughter as praise of you.
All	God of Laughter, give us joy.
Leader	God of Laughter, help us delight in our humanness.
All	God of Laughter, give us joy.
Leader	God of Laughter, may we reflect your own laughter.
All	God of Laughter, give us joy.
Leader	God of Laughter, we trust in your victory and ours. We believe that all shall be well.
All	God of Laughter, give us joy.

READING: *Matthew 5:1–12*

Eight children carry signs labeled with the names of the blessed in the Beatitudes: the poor in spirit, those who mourn, the meek, those who hunger and thirst for righteousness, the merciful, the pure in heart, peacemakers, and the persecuted. As the Beatitude is read, a halo is put on the child's head or a star pinned to the shoulder to indicate the kingdom is theirs.

Narrator	When Jesus saw the crowds, he went up the mountain; and after he sat down, his disciples came to him. Then he began to speak, and taught them, saying:
Reader 1	Blessed are the poor in spirit, for theirs is the kingdom of heaven. (*pause*)
Reader 2	Blessed are those who mourn, for they will be comforted. (*pause*)
Reader 3	Blessed are the meek, for they will inherit the earth. (*pause*)
Reader 4	Blessed are those who hunger and thirst for righteousness, for they will be filled. (*pause*)
Reader 5	Blessed are the merciful, for they will receive mercy. (*pause*)
Reader 6	Blessed are the pure in heart, for they will see God. (*pause*)
Reader 7	Blessed are the peacemakers, for they will be called children of God. (*pause*)
Reader 8	Blessed are those who are persecuted for righteousness' sake, for theirs is the kingdom of heaven. (*pause*)
Narrator	Blessed are you when people revile you and persecute you and utter all kinds of evil against you falsely on my account. Rejoice and be glad, for your reward is great in heaven.

REFLECTION

Start with a laughing contest. See who can make others laugh. When the ribs can't take it any longer, quiet the group to begin the rest of the prayer.

Laughter is good. Laughter brings us closer to our real selves; therefore, it brings us closer to God. Children laugh easily, and the kingdom of God is for children, those who laugh easily. The Book of Ecclesiastes tells us that "For everything there is a season, and a time for every matter under heaven: …a time to weep, and a time to laugh" (Eccl 3:1, 4).

Mardi Gras is the time to laugh. Why laugh on this day? Our first thought may focus on partying and eating rich foods before the fasting of Lent arrives. But the laughter goes deeper. Christians know that no matter how difficult and sorrowful life may become, the end of the journey is heaven. Our life story ends with laughter, because the life story of Jesus ends with laughter.

Jesus had the last laugh. As Jesus walked to Calvary, was crucified, died and was buried, the devils thought they had won. Can you hear their fiendish laughter, as they call to one another: "We got him! He's dead now. No more Jesus-do-gooder! No more talk of the kingdom of heaven. No more telling people to love their enemies. Ha-ha-ha! We must admit Jesus put up a good fight; he never gave into all our tempting. He never said or did anything the slightest bit evil. But Jesus is in our kingdom now—the kingdom of death, decay, and oblivion. Ha-ha-ha!"

The devils didn't know the end of the story, but we do. Jesus rose triumphant from the grave. Laughing, Jesus ascended in glory. Laughing, Jesus sent his Spirit. Laughing, Jesus reigns supreme over the entire universe. God laughs, and we laugh. Not the laughter of fiends and fools. God's laughter and ours is childlike, confident, carefree, and blessed. God's laughter puts beauty and goodness into creation and grace into our souls. We are told, "Blessed are they who mourn, for they shall laugh." That is our promise. Good things can always follow bad things, because the resurrection of Jesus followed his death.

SHARING

▶ Do you think of God as a God of Laughter? Why or why not? Do you see God as someone who delights in us and the rest of creation?

▶ Share your knowledge of the origins of Mardi Gras. Does Mardi Gras help you enter into the season of Lent?

▶ Share occasions when good things followed bad things, as well as your reaction.

▶ Which Beatitude do you find most comforting? most confusing? most true to your own spirituality or experiences? most lacking in our world?

▶ If you could wave a magic wand and everyone in the world would immediately begin practicing one Beatitude, which one would it be? Why?

ACTION STEP

Prepare a personal plan for Lent or a plan for your family or group. Consider including prayer, fasting, and almsgiving that will help transform you into Christ, the purpose of undergoing lenten conversion.

Observe Lent by being attentive to one Beatitude each week. List ways to live the Beatitude.

Whatever you do, do it in Christ's name. This includes parties. As you plan your next party, begin with prayer, and reflect upon ways the party can become a loving, unifying occasion.

CLOSING PRAYER

Prepare a PowerPoint presentation of beautiful scenery. As participants watch, ask them to think about God's laughter as God created the universe. Let the prayer be a simple, silent "song" of gratitude from the depths of one's heart.

OPTIONAL ACTIVITIES FOR FAMILIES AND GROUPS

1. February is sometimes a dull, dreary month. As a family or group, prepare an activity that is fun for yourselves and others: euchre tournament for the neighborhood, talent show presented for the elderly or ill, finger painting in pudding for little ones, or something else.

2. Using the lectionary, find the gospel readings for the Sundays of Lent. Draw a picture of each reading. Post one picture each week on the refrigerator.

3. If Mardi Gras falls near Valentine's Day, use a Concordance to the Bible to locate the word "heart." Select some Scripture quotations with the word "heart" to make homemade Valentine cards or placemats.

Take Up Your Cross

– LENT –

BEFORE YOU BEGIN

Materials: (optional) Cross or crucifix and purple cloth

To do: Assign readers and leaders for the game "Follow the Leader"

SONG

Song with theme of Lent, cross, or discipleship

OPENING PRAYER

Leader	Father of mercy, you have given us your Son.
All	Thank you for giving us your Son.
Leader	Father, you accepted your Son's sacrifice on the cross as a perfect gift, which saved us.
All	Thank you for giving us your Son.
Leader	Father, accept our sacrifices with the sacrifice of your Son.
All	Thank you for giving us your Son. Help us to take up our cross as Jesus did.

READING: *Luke 9:21–25*

Narrator Jesus said,

Jesus The Son of Man must undergo great suffering, and be rejected by the elders, chief priests, and scribes, and be killed, and on the third day be raised.

Narrator Then he said to them all,

Jesus If any want to become my followers, let them deny themselves and take up their cross daily and follow me. For those who want to save their life will lose it, and those who lose their life for my sake will save it. What does it profit them if they gain the whole world, but lose or forfeit themselves?

REFLECTION

Youngest children are asked to demonstrate the game Follow the Leader. Let at least two children have a chance to lead.

(*Question directed to children*) Which do you like better: leading or following? Why? (*Question directed to all participants*) Which do you like better: leading or following? Today we will follow our leader Jesus Christ, but it is not a game. It is quite serious. Jesus tells us that if we follow him, we will need to pick up our cross. To be a disciple of Jesus means that we have to be ready to suffer.

Let children demonstrate following Jesus who carries his cross. Then ask the leader representing Jesus to leave the room momentarily.

Because Jesus is not on earth, someone else needs to lead. Who does the leading now? We lead when we are willing to pick up our cross. We must do now what Jesus did when he was on earth. Why? We are the representatives of Jesus Christ today in our town, our school, our place of work.

SHARING

▶ What do you think Jesus meant when he told us to deny ourselves, take up our crosses, and follow him?

▶ Jesus took upon himself our sins and suffered for our guilt. Do you ever take upon yourself the problems of others? What happens when you do this?

▶ Jesus saw that his death was coming. How do you cope with the knowledge that death is coming for you, your friends, your family?

▶ Lent is a time for giving up (sacrificing) and giving (almsgiving) and praying. What are some things to sacrifice? What are some ways to give? How might you pray this Lent?

ACTION STEP

Decide upon three things you can do during Lent to be a better follower of Jesus.

Do something to take away another's burdens (examples: free service, errands).

CLOSING PRAYER

Leader   Let us stand in a circle and pass the crucifix around, each one holding it for a few seconds. The group will pray for the one holding the crucifix that he or she may take up his or her cross this Lent and become an even better follower of Jesus.

Instrumental background music may be added

OPTIONAL ACTIVITIES FOR FAMILIES OR GROUPS

1. Make a cross from poster board or felt. Put an image of Jesus on one side and yourself on the other to remind yourself that you follow Jesus when shouldering your cross.

2. Make a list of Lenten activities that your family or group could do. Include parish activities, such as penance service, Way of the Cross, adoration.

Feast of the Institution of the Eucharist

– HOLY THURSDAY –

BEFORE YOU BEGIN

Materials: (optional) picture of Last Supper, loaf of bread, wine (red-colored water), towel and basin

To do: assign readers

SONG

Theme appropriate for Holy Thursday, Eucharist

OPENING PRAYER

Leader   Anticipating his death on the cross and resurrection from the dead, Jesus gave us his Body to eat and his Blood to drink.

Melody: Refrain of "On Eagles' Wings" (Michael Joncas)

All   (*sung*) And we proclaim his death until he comes,
When we eat the Meal of Love.
Source of our life and sum of faith,
We gather in the name of Christ, Bread of Life.

READING: *Luke 22:14–15, 19–20*

Narrator   When the hour came, Jesus took his place at the table, and the apostles with him. He said to them,

Jesus   I have eagerly desired to eat this Passover with you before I suffer; for I tell you, I will not eat it until it is fulfilled in the kingdom of God.

Narrator   Then he took a loaf of bread, and when he had given thanks, he broke it and gave it to them, saying,

Jesus   This is my body, which is given for you. Do this in remembrance of me.

Narrator   And he did the same with the cup after supper, saying,

Jesus   This cup that is poured out for you is the new covenant in my blood.

REFLECTION *(At the asterisk participants may say, "We become what we eat.")*

Holy Thursday begins the Easter Triduum, the Sacred Three Days, the holiest time of the year for Christians. We focus on the most important events in the life of Jesus. We begin with the Last Supper when Jesus gave us himself as spiritual food.* The disciples ate the Body and Blood of our Lord.* When we receive Eucharist, we eat the Body and Blood of Jesus.* When we gather at the Table of the Lord to hear his Word and eat his Sacrament, we remember the death of the Lord.* Jesus will come back, and then we will be gathered at a banquet in heaven.* During this sacred time let us speak and live the way Jesus would.*

SHARING

▶ What does the Eucharist mean for you?

▶ There are many names for the Eucharist, such as the Breaking of the Bread, the memorial of the Lord's Passion and Resurrection, the Holy Sacrifice of the Mass, the Blessed Sacrament, sacrament of unity, sacrament of salvation, sacrifice of praise, foretaste of the heavenly banquet, Viaticum, and others. Do any of these titles have special significance to you?

▶ How do you make each Mass special so that its rituals do not become routine?

▶ What does it mean for you to say that we become what we eat when we receive Holy Communion?

▶ How can you make the Sacred Three Days a holy time?

ACTION STEP

Plan how to make the Easter Triduum a special time. Consider attending all the liturgies, reading the Passion Narratives at home, being quiet during the hours when Jesus hung upon the cross, or avoiding unnecessary work and entertainment.

Challenge yourself to extend the presence of Christ in your home, neighborhood, or place of work whenever you leave the Holy Sacrifice of the Eucharist.

Deepen bonds with families and friends by making meals occasions of unity by deeper conversation.

CLOSING PRAYER
(Participants hold hands and make a circle around the symbols of Eucharist)

Leader   The response is "Thank you, Jesus, Bread of Life."
For the Eucharist, the source of our Christian life, (R)
For the unity that comes from the Eucharist, (R)
For the memorial of the Lord's Passion and Resurrection, (R)
For the Holy Spirit who changes bread and wine into the Body and Blood of Christ, (R)
For the Holy Spirit who changes us into the Body and Blood of Christ, (R)
For the Eucharist in which all creation is presented to the Father in a sacrifice of praise for all the good things God has made, (R)
For the Eucharist in which we are united with Christ in prayer and praise, (R)
For the Sacred Three Days that are the climax of the Church Year, (R)

OPTIONAL ACTIVITIES FOR FAMILIES AND GROUPS

1. Spend time before the Altar of Repose on Holy Thursday night. Pray for an intention important to your family or group.

2. Discuss or demonstrate how bread is made, and compare the steps to the Eucharist; for example, the wheat seeds die, many grains of wheat are needed to make one loaf, and bread gives nourishment.

3. Make a three-part poster representing the historical events of the first Holy Thursday, Good Friday, and Holy Saturday.

4. When decorating Easter eggs, include religious symbols.

Commemoration of Our Lord's Passion and Death

– GOOD FRIDAY –

BEFORE YOU BEGIN

Materials: (optional) symbols of the passion and death of Jesus, such as crucifix, nails, crown of thorns, dice, red cloth

To do: assign readers and groups to make tableaus

SONG

Theme appropriate for Good Friday

OPENING PRAYER

Leader   Jesus humbled himself and became obedient unto death, even death on a cross.

All   Lord Jesus Christ, King of Glory, you made the cross of death the Tree of Life. Whenever we look at the cross, let us praise you for your sacrifice that redeemed the world. From your death, eternal life has come. We adore you, O Christ, and we praise you, because by your holy cross you have redeemed the world.

READING: *Luke 23:26–28, 32–34, 39–46*

Narrator 1   As they led Jesus away, they seized a man, Simon of Cyrene, who was coming from the country, and they laid the cross on him, and made him carry it behind Jesus.

Narrator 2	A great number of the people followed him, and among there were women who were wailing for him. But Jesus turned to them and said,
Jesus	Daughters of Jerusalem, do not weep for me, but weep for yourselves and for your children.
Narrator 3	Two others also, who were criminals, were led away to be put to death with him. When they came to the place that is called The Skull, they crucified Jesus there with the criminals, one on his right and one on his left. Then Jesus said,
Jesus	Father, forgive them; for they do not know what they are doing.
Narrator 1	One of the criminals who was hanged there kept deriding him and saying,
Criminal 1	Are you not the Messiah? Save yourself and us!
Narrator 2	But the other rebuked him, saying,
Criminal 2	Do you not fear God, since you are under the same sentence of condemnation? And we indeed have been condemned justly, for we are getting what we deserve for our deeds, but this man has done nothing wrong.
Narrator 3	Then he said,
Criminal 2	Jesus, remember me when you come into your kingdom.
Narrator 1	He replied,
Jesus	Truly I tell you, today you will be with me in Paradise.
Narrator 2	It was now about noon, and darkness came over the whole land until three in the afternoon, while the sun's light failed; and the curtain of the temple was torn in two. Then Jesus, crying with a loud voice, said,
Jesus	Father, into your hands I commend my spirit.
Narrator 3	Having said this, he breathed his last.

REFLECTION

Before the leader gives the reflection, small groups are asked to create the following tableaux: (1) Jesus with the weeping women, (2) Simon of Cyrene and Jesus, (3) Jesus and the Good Thief, (4) Mary and John standing beneath the cross, and (5) Jesus praying to his Father. As the leader talks, he or she walks from one tableau to another as they are numbered.

Jesus did all that he could do for us. He spent his life showing us how to live. He died showing us how to die. Jesus died forgiving his apostles who abandoned him and forgiving those who crucified him. (1) On his way to Calvary he extended compassion to the weeping women. (2) Jesus humbly accepted the help of Simon of Cyrene. (3) Jesus died promising heaven to the Good Thief. (4) Jesus died making sure his mother, Mary, would be cared for by his loved apostle John. (5) Above all, Jesus died by giving himself completely in love and offering himself to the Father. Right before he gave up his spirit, Jesus said, "Father, into your hands I commend my spirit" (Lk 23:46).

In all these ways as Jesus relates to others, we learn the meaning of the crucifixion. (1) We learn that we will undoubtedly suffer as followers of Jesus, just as the weeping women would suffer for themselves and their children. (2) We learn the proper attitude toward suffering, that we should pick up our crosses as Simon of Cyrene did. (3) We learn that salvation is for everyone, even for a thief who acknowledged that Jesus was not a criminal but rather a king with a spiritual kingdom. (4) We learn that we need to think of others and not become self-centered when we're suffering, as Jesus asked John to take care of his mother. (5) Above all, we learn to give our whole being over to God, to let our life and death be totally lived according to God's will.

SHARING

▶ Which aspect of the passion and death of Jesus holds the most emotion for you?

▶ Do you feel like any person in the Passion Narrative: the criminals, the weeping women, the apostles, Simon of Cyrene, a passer-by, a soldier, Mary or Jesus? Why?

▶ Although Jesus feels abandoned by his Father, the Father and Spirit are involved in Jesus' passion and death. How?

▶ How have you made or how will you make Holy Week a special time of spiritual growth?

▶ Are you afraid to die? How can the passion of Jesus give you courage?

ACTION STEP

Be attentive to those who have lost loved ones over the past months. Encourage them to share stories of those who have died, or tell them that you are thinking of them as their grief continues.

Attend the liturgy of Good Friday. If you are not able to, meditate on the Passion Narratives.

Give the cross a prominent place in your home. Decorate it in a way that reminds you that the cross is our hope.

CLOSING PRAYER *(Participant holds a cross high.)*

Leader	Behold the cross on which hung the Savior of the world.
All	Come, let us worship.
Leader	Behold the cross on which our sins were laid.
All	Come, let us worship.
Leader	Behold the cross carried by Jesus who made it the Tree of Life.
All	Come, let us worship.
Leader	Behold the cross before which all kneel: the rich and the poor, the lonely and abandoned, people who are joyful and people who are sad, widows and mothers who have lost their

children, friends and lovers, little children and the elderly, people in prison, refugees fleeing for safety, migrants far from home, students and teachers, all of us here and across the globe who know where grace comes from, who know that salvation hangs upon the cross.

All   Come, let us worship.

OPTIONAL ACTIVITIES FOR FAMILIES AND GROUPS

1. On a long roll of paper draw the scenes of one of the Passion Narratives. Perhaps draw more than one Passion Narrative to compare them.

2. Watch a religious program on television, and discuss it as a family or group.

3. Eat very simple meals during Holy Week remembering those who live the Passion of Jesus in their daily hunger and malnutrition. Or give up snacks and sweets.

4. Walk through your home noting the religious symbols and "see them for the first time again." If there are few such symbols, consider obtaining more.

Hunting for Jesus

- EASTER -

BEFORE YOU BEGIN

Materials: plastic or real Easter eggs

To do: hide eggs; ask youth to lead the cheers that are the opening prayer; assign readers

SONG

Easter song

OPENING PRAYER *(Cheers led by cheerleaders)*

V-I-C-T-O-R-Y!

Christ is lifted up on high!

He has risen from the grave.

Grace is ours! We know we're saved!

Roll that stone! Roll it away!

Jesus Christ lives today!

Are we risen up with Him?

Yes, we are. Heaven we win!

Are we on the winning team?
Yes, we're on the winning team.
Do you know He rose on high?
Yes, we know He rose on high.

Jesus lives!
Jesus lives!
New life's begun.
New life's begun
Yea, Jesus!

READING: *John 20:1–9*

Reader 1	Early on the first day of the week, while it was still dark, Mary Magdalene came to the tomb and saw that the stone had been removed from the tomb. So she ran and went to Simon Peter and the other disciple, the one whom Jesus loved, and said to them.
Mary	They have taken the Lord out of the tomb, and we do not know where they have laid him.
Reader 2	Then Peter and the other disciple set out and went toward the tomb. The two were running together, but the other disciple outran Peter and reached the tomb first.
Reader 3	He bent down to look in and saw the linen wrappings lying there, but he did not go in. Then Simon Peter came, following him, and went into the tomb. He saw the linen wrappings lying there, and the cloth that had been on Jesus' head, not lying with the linen wrappings but rolled up in a place by itself.
Reader 4	Then the other disciple, who reached the tomb first, also went in, and he saw and believed; for as yet they did not understand the scripture, that he must rise from the dead. Then the disciples returned to their homes.

REFLECTION *(Children participate in an Easter egg hunt)*

Mary Magdalene looked for Jesus on the first day of the week. She went to the tomb to be near the dead body of her friend Jesus. He wasn't there! She thought the body must have been stolen, so she ran to tell the apostles. Peter and John ran to the tomb, but they didn't find Jesus either! They began to believe that Jesus rose from the dead as he said he would.

You found the eggs, because they were somewhere around to be found. Jesus was raised to his Father's throne in glory. He passed from death to life, from the cruelest suffering on the cross to the greatest glory in heaven. But Jesus let himself be found. The resurrection of Jesus meant that Jesus could always be found. The resurrection meant that Jesus would always have a glorious body filled with the power of the Holy Spirit. Not held back by space and time, Jesus in his glorified body could always be present wherever Jesus wanted to be. And where does Jesus want to be? Jesus wants to be with us in so many ways: in the Eucharist, in his Word, and in one another. If we look for him, it won't be hard to find him. Because of the resurrection Jesus is always right there.

SHARING

▶ Where do you look for Jesus? Do you find him there?

▶ Why is Easter the most important feast of the year?

▶ Jesus completed his mission. He reigns forever as the Victor. How do you share in the victory of Jesus over sin and death?

ACTION STEP

Decide how you can continue Easter joy throughout the fifty-day season.

Welcome the new members of the Church who were baptized or made a profession of faith at the Easter Vigil.

Make efforts to find Christ in those persons and situations where Christ seems to be "hiding."

CLOSING PRAYER

Leader   The response is "Thank you, Risen Lord."
            For rising from the dead, (R)
            For entering heaven and constantly praying for us there, (R)
            For keeping your wounds in your glorified body, (R)
            For being with us always, (R)
            For pouring out your Spirit upon us, (R)
            For promising us that we would live forever with you, (R)
            For your promise that you will come again in glory, (R)
            For the joy of the Easter Season, (R)

OPTIONAL ACTIVITIES FOR FAMILIES AND GROUPS

1. During Lent we make Lenten resolutions. Make some Easter resolutions that focus on being happy, giving joy to others, or living the gifts of the Holy Spirit.

2. Research Easter customs or the origin of the name "Easter."

3. Share Easter goodies with someone who is lonely.

Dying to Live

– EASTER SEASON –

BEFORE YOU BEGIN

Materials: Easter goodies, such as candy, cookies, cupcakes, or bookmarks

To do: Assign and practice parts for the dramatized reading.

SONG

Theme of Easter, peace, or life

OPENING PRAYER

Leader   The response is "We believe."
          Risen Lord, you died for our sins. (R)
          Risen Lord, your dying and rising fulfilled your mission on earth. (R)
          Risen Lord, you rose victorious from the grave. (R)
          Risen Lord, you live beyond time and space. (R)
          Risen Lord, you share your risen life with us. (R)
          Risen Lord, you are with us always. (R)
          Risen Lord, because of you life follows death. (R)

READING: *John 20:19–29*

Reader 1	When it was evening on that day, the first day of the week, and the doors of the house where the disciples had met were locked for fear of the Jews, Jesus came and stood among them and said,
Jesus	Peace be with you.
Reader 2	After he said this, he showed them his hands and his side. Then the disciples rejoiced when they saw the Lord. Jesus said to them again,
Jesus	Peace be with you. As the Father has sent me, so I send you.
Reader 3	When he had said this, he breathed on them and said to them,
Jesus	Receive the Holy Spirit. If you forgive the sins of any, they are forgiven them; if you retain the sins of any, they are retained.
Reader 4	But Thomas (who was called the Twin), one of the twelve, was not with them when Jesus came. So the other disciples told him,
Disciples	We have seen the Lord.
Reader 1	But he said to them,
Thomas	Unless I see the mark of the nails in his hands, and put my finger in the mark of the nails and my hand in his side, I will not believe.
Reader 2	A week later his disciples were again in the house, and Thomas was with them. Although the doors were shut, Jesus came and stood among them and said,
Jesus	Peace be with you.
Reader 3	Then he said to Thomas,
Jesus	Put your finger here and see my hands. Reach out your hand and put it in my side. Do not doubt but believe.
Reader 4	Thomas answered him,
Thomas	My Lord and my God!
Reader 1	Jesus said to him,
Jesus	Have you believed because you have seen me? Blessed are those who have not seen and yet have come to believe.

REFLECTION

Jesus suffered terribly, and he chose to keep the wounds of the nails and spear so that we will always remember his death on the cross. All the angels and saints in heaven see the wounded Christ now in glory. Jesus is victorious over sin, suffering, and death. Through death, Jesus rose to new life. We will do the same. When we die, the way we live changes. We will live more fully. We will be even more alive. On earth people suffer, endure trials, and die. These hardships may last days, months, or years. But in heaven there will be happiness forever. That is the promise of Easter. We die to live. Life follows death.

Springtime reminds us, too, that life follows death. Seeds die in the ground in order to rise above the ground with flowers or grain. A tree that appears dead suddenly bursts forth with buds and leaves and fruit. Spring is the year's big breakthrough, and the resurrection is God's big breakthrough on earth. The fullness of God's life is ours today and forever.

SHARING

▶ When have you experienced new life through suffering or death? What reminds you that life follows death?

▶ Eternal life is not only in the future. It is ours now through grace. How do you experience eternal life now?

▶ Do you think our "wounds" (sickness, limitations, weaknesses, sorrow) will be part of us in heaven?

▶ Jesus gave peace on Easter. Why do you think Jesus made peace his Easter gift? How do you find peace in your life? How do you bring peace to others?

▶ If you were with the disciples behind the locked doors, how do you think you would have reacted to the appearance of Jesus?

ACTION STEP

Bring peace to a situation where there is conflict.

Memorize the Peace Prayer of Saint Francis.

Help heal someone's emotional wounds.

Take care of Planet Earth wounded by pollution and misuse.

CLOSING PRAYER

Sit in a circle and pass a platter of Easter goodies. As you turn to the next person, wish them Easter peace: "May Easter peace be with you," or "May life follow death."

OPTIONAL ACTIVITIES FOR FAMILIES AND GROUPS

Consider planting a garden and be reminded as you care for it throughout the Easter Season and beyond that life follows death.

God-with-Us

- THE ASCENSION -

BEFORE YOU BEGIN

Materials: (optional) Globe or representation of the universe, flowers or plants, Easter candle

SONG

Song with theme of Ascension, creation, or praise

OPENING PRAYER

Leader	Let us pray that our Father in heaven will take us to heaven as he did his son Jesus.
All	Our Father in heaven, we want to be with you and Jesus forever.
Leader	We praise you, Risen and Ascended Lord.
All	We praise you as King of all creation. You are the Power behind the whole Universe.

READING: *Matthew 28:16–20*

Now the eleven disciples went to Galilee, to the mountain to which Jesus had directed them. When they saw him, they worshiped him; but some doubted. And Jesus came and said to them, "All authority in heaven and on earth has been given to me. Go therefore and make disciples of all nations, baptizing them in the name of the Father and of the Son and of the Holy Spirit, and teaching them to obey everything that I have commanded you. And remember, I am with you always, to the end of the age."

REFLECTION

As the leader reads the reflection, the group may respond after each "Why?" with "Jesus put his heart among us." Perhaps add gestures, such as covering one's heart.

Sometimes when we think of Jesus' ascension into heaven, we think that he moved away from us. But it is impossible for God to do that, because God wants to be close to us. This special day of the Ascension means that Jesus let his heart flow down into this earth. When Jesus became human, he became just like us. He lived to the full and died to the full. Why? **JESUS PUT HIS HEART AMONG US.** When Jesus was taken into heaven, he took all his humanness and all created things with him. Why? **JESUS PUT HIS HEART AMONG US.** All the saints and angels in heaven see God in God's glory. In a heavenly way the Jesus who lived in Nazareth lives forever, just as friends and relatives of ours who died live forever. They see Jesus face-to-face, and so will we when we're in heaven. Meanwhile, we have the privilege of continuing the work of Jesus on earth. Why? **JESUS PUT HIS HEART AMONG US.** God planned that everyone would be saved. God even wants the whole world to share in God's glory. Why? **JESUS PUT HIS HEART AMONG US.** We need to continue the work of salvation. This may be difficult, but Jesus promised to be with us. When he ascended to the Father, he told us, "I am with you always to the end of the age" (Mt 28:20). Why? **JESUS PUT HIS HEART AMONG US.** Because God is always with us, we can do what Jesus did: we can let our hearts be involved with everyone and everything. We can bring all creation before the throne of God. Some day God's plan for the world will be completed and beautiful and perfect. Why? **JESUS PUT HIS HEART AMONG US.**

SHARING

▶ Is there something from the reflection or reading that touched you?

▶ When you pray, how do you imagine God—in heaven, with us on earth, other?

▶ When you think of redemption, do you feel yourself redeemed? Do you see the world as redeemed? Do you have a role in redeeming the world? How?

▶ Do you realize that God is with us always? How can you try to remember God's presence more frequently?

▶ Jesus is the head of creation and has entrusted the care of the earth to us. How are you caring for the earth?

▶ The Easter Season is coming to a close with the celebration of the Ascension and Pentecost. How have you tried to celebrate the resurrection through this fifty-day season?

ACTION STEP

What action do you plan to live in response to this sharing?

Put your heart into everything you do. Be conscious of the life and love that is in the universe and in you, and realize that all creation will reach its fullness in Christ, the Head of Creation.

CLOSING

Leader   Let us pray that the fullness of redemption given us in Jesus Christ will come to the whole universe.

Suggestion: A young person might hold up the globe or symbol of the universe

Leader   Risen Lord, the fullness of your heart is still with us here on earth.

All   We praise you, Risen Lord, for your love.

Leader   Risen Lord, you took on our humanness.

All   We praise you, Risen Lord, for being just like us.

Leader   Risen Lord, you continue creation in us.

All   We praise you, Risen Lord, for permitting us to take care of your earth.

Leader   Risen Lord, your plan of creation continues until its fullness is reached in you.

All   Help us be open to your plan. Let our love flow deeply in care of Earth.

Leader   Let us bring all creation before the throne of God.

All   Risen Lord, we unite ourselves with all creation and present ourselves before you. We praise you, we thank you, we adore you. Thank you for entrusting us with continuing your plan for all creation. Thank you for being with us always.

OPTIONAL ACTIVITIES FOR FAMILIES OR GROUPS

1. Draw a picture showing that God takes care of the world and wants us to do the same.

2. Make a plan to help the environment and work on it together.

3. The Solemnity of the Ascension occurs in the season of weddings, First Communions, and graduations. As you bless the persons celebrating these events, remind them that they are part of God's plan for the world.

Gifts Galore!

– PENTECOST –

BEFORE YOU BEGIN

Materials: Easter candle and seven small candles or vigil lights labeled with names of the Spirit's gifts

To do: Make signs with the names of the seven gifts of the Holy Spirit

SONG

Song about the Holy Spirit or the Spirit's gifts

OPENING PRAYER

When the leader prays, members of the group light the corresponding candle using light from the Easter candle to show that the Spirit is the Spirit of Jesus, the Risen Lord's Easter gift to us.

Leader	Come, Spirit of Wisdom.
All	Come, Holy Spirit, come!
Leader	Come, Spirit of Understanding.
All	Come, Holy Spirit, come!

Leader	Come, Spirit of Knowledge,
All	Come, Holy Spirit, come!
Leader	Come, Spirit of Courage,
All	Come, Holy Spirit, come!
Leader	Come, Spirit of Right Judgment,
All	Come, Holy Spirit, come!
Leader	Come, Spirit of Reverence,
All	Come, Holy Spirit, come!
Leader	Come, Spirit of Awe and Wonder!
All	Come, Holy Spirit, come!

READING: *1 Corinthians 12:4–11*

Now there are varieties of gifts, but the same Spirit; and there are varieties of services, but the same Lord; and there are varieties of activities, but it is the same God who activates all of them in everyone. To each is given the manifestation of the Spirit for the common good. To one is given through the Spirit the utterance of wisdom, and to another the utterance of knowledge according to the same Spirit, to another faith by the same Spirit, to another gifts of healing by the one Spirit, to another the working of miracles, to another prophecy, to another the discernment of spirits, to another various kinds of tongues, to another the interpretation of tongues. All these are activated by one and the same Spirit, who allots to each one individually just as the Spirit chooses.

REFLECTION *(Children may whisper the word "gifts" at the asterisk.)*

Pentecost ends the Easter Season. Pentecost completes the work of Jesus. Now it is the Holy Spirit's turn to continue the work of creation and redemption. It's our turn now, too.* On the first Pentecost the Holy Spirit came into the world, into the Church. The Spirit came to us, too, at our Baptism. The Spirit is always with us on big days like First Communion and Confirmation. The Spirit is with us on all the other days, too. God is ours!* God gives us more than just the gifts of the Spirit. God gives us the Spirit! This is so wonderful that we have been celebrating Easter for fifty days.* Because God is so awesome, so big, we try to understand the Big Gift that is God by remembering the little gifts that belong to God. God shares the Big Gift—Himself! And God shares the little gifts: charity, joy, peace. And many more. There are loads of gifts written about in the New Testament: wisdom, knowledge, faith, healing, prophecy, and more. And our own lives tell us that God gives people gifts: encouragement, hospitality, music, craftsmanship, sharing with the poor, and many more. And the gifts keep on coming! Gifts galore!*

SHARING

▶ Which gifts of the Holy Spirit do you or others in your group possess?

▶ As you look back to the Easter Triduum, was it the high point of the church year for you? Are you celebrating Christ's resurrection throughout the fifty days?

▶ Which gift of the Holy Spirit do you want most? Could this gift be already at work within you?

ACTION STEP

Decide upon a service project using the Spirit-given gifts of the group.

Write a note of gratitude to persons in your church for using their gifts.

Pray for the courage to spread your faith in the Risen Lord.

If you are unfamiliar with the charismatic movement, do some research or invite a speaker.

Prepare a charismatic prayer experience.

CLOSING

Leader Let us pray that the Spirit may energize us to become more alive in the Risen Lord and more active in the Church.

All Bountiful Spirit, give us your gifts. Help us to receive them and use them. Build up your holy people in love and unity, that we may witness the goodness of God. Make our lives examples of Christ in our world today. Thank you for your gifts. We dare to ask for more—gifts galore.

OPTIONAL ACTIVITIES FOR FAMILIES OR GROUPS

1. As a family take the time to tell one another the gifts they see in one another and thank them for using their gifts. Perhaps do this at a special meal.

2. As a group, discover a need in your area (example: assisted living, soup kitchen, literacy program, migrant camps) and commit yourselves to help.

3. Do something fun together to conclude the festivities of the great fifty days (examples: picnic, afternoon in a park, sing-along, movie, visiting).

4. Write gifts of the Spirit on cards and put them into a box. Each member of the group pulls a card to practice that gift in the coming week.

A Pebble in a Pond

BEFORE YOU BEGIN

Materials: container of water and pebbles

To do: Assign readers

SONG

Theme of sharing

OPENING PRAYER

Leader   The response is "Help us share."

                When members of our families need something, (R)

                When our church calls us to work together, (R)

                When collections are taken at work, in school, or in our neighborhood, (R)

                When we hear of natural disasters, (R)

                When people need a helping hand, (R)

                When friends need a listening ear, (R)

                When we would rather keep our money, time, and talent to ourselves, (R)

READING: *Mark 12:41–44*

Narrator   Jesus sat down opposite the treasury, and watched the crowd putting money into the treasury. Many rich people put in large sums. A poor widow came and put in two small copper coins, which are worth a penny. Then he called his disciples and said to them,

Jesus   Truly I tell you, this poor widow has put in more than all those who are contributing to the treasury. For all of them have contributed out of their abundance; but she out of her poverty has put in everything she had, all she had to live on.

REFLECTION
(Young persons toss some pebbles into a container of water to watch ripples.)

Tossing pebbles into water creates rings. In a pond the rings may even reach the opposite shore. Pebbles seem small, but they have impact. The poor widow tossed into the treasury two small copper coins, the way we might give a couple of pennies at the cashier line. Both she and we make some impact, because little things add up. But beyond the financial value is the sharing of our heart. The poor widow gave from her livelihood; she gave what she needed for survival, not the pennies that would make her purse weigh less. Whenever we give money or time or talent from our surplus or from what we could really use ourselves, we make a ripple effect. Other people's lives are touched. There's more money for research, the handicap ramp is built faster, the park or interior of a house is made more beautiful. And the ripples of these good deeds continue to reach farther shores. Good deeds tend to multiply, as people see our good deeds and say, "Why, I can do that, too!" And the recipients of our money, time, and talent are encouraged to keep the goodness rippling.

SHARING

▶   Why do you think Jesus pointed out this woman? What would you have said about her?

▶   What is your response to requests for your money, time, or talent? Why?

▶   When did you do something small or give something small but realized its big impact?

ACTION STEP

Determine a need that could use the money, time, and talent of your church. Make a plan of action to involve as many members as possible.

Resolve to contribute to those standing near store entrances.

Surprise someone with a good deed (visit to a lonely person, cooked meal for a harried parent, cleaning or lawn work for someone incapacitated).

CLOSING PRAYER

Leader   Jesus, you told us that what we do to others we do to you. Help us become aware of the needs of others and help them. Make us like the poor widow who was willing to give from her necessity. Make our desire to live the gospel so strong that our lives will have an impact on others. May our good deeds have a ripple effect, spreading goodness according to your plan.

OPTIONAL ACTIVITIES FOR FAMILIES OR GROUPS

1. Go to a pond and drop in pebbles. Note the effects and apply them to your life.

2. To raise money for a good cause, drop coins in a bottle by standing, putting the coin under your nose and aiming for the opening in the neck of the bottle. For every ten cents that lands in the bottle, the player receives a piece of candy. All money in and around the bottle is given to a worthy cause.

3. Join another family or group to prepare a backyard festival or festival in the park with very simple games like ping pong and bean bag tosses. Entrance fee is a donation to a good cause, and the prize is simply having fun and a treat at the end of the allotted time.

Go on Your Way. I Am Sending You

BEFORE YOU BEGIN

Materials: magazine pictures cut into puzzle pieces, Scripture verses on cards

To do: Write Scripture verses on the theme of discipleship or missionary spirit on cards or pieces of paper. Assign readers. Cut magazine pictures into two puzzle pieces, enough for everyone to have a puzzle piece.

SONG

Theme: discipleship, evangelization, kingdom of God

OPENING PRAYER *(To be read by a child)*

Jesus, you couldn't tell everyone about your Father and your Holy Spirit. You needed helpers. You asked seventy persons to go out and tell everyone they could find about your good Father and your Holy Spirit. Even today some people do not know you. We pray for those people who do not follow you or even know you. Help them learn about you. Help us tell others about you, too.

READING: *Luke 10:1–3, 8–9*

Reader   The Lord appointed seventy others and sent them on ahead of him in pairs to every town and place where he himself intended to go. He said to them,

Jesus   The harvest is plentiful, but the laborers are few; therefore ask the Lord of the harvest to send out laborers into his harvest. Go on your way. See, I am sending you out like lambs into the midst of wolves….Whatever house you enter, first say, "Peace to this house!"… Whenever you enter a town and its people welcome you, eat what is set before you; cure the sick who are there, and say to them, "The kingdom of God has come near to you."

REFLECTION
(With a syncopated beat and arm gestures, say "Jesus needs us" at the asterisk.)

Cut magazine pictures into two puzzle pieces. Everyone in the group receives a puzzle piece and needs to find the other half. When that person is found, sit together for the rest of the time.

Even though Jesus was God, as a human he was limited. Jesus could be in only one place, he could only teach the people in one location, he could work miracles only where persons believed and brought him sick persons to cure.* Jesus was so great, he influenced the whole world. Yet he still needed helpers to spread the Good News.* Jesus needs us to continue the healing.* Jesus needs us to bring about the kingdom here on earth.* In this story Jesus appointed seventy helpers.* They were to take the peace of Jesus and bring it with them into every house.* Today Jesus still needs us.* Jesus needs us to share what we have with those in need.* Jesus needs us to tell others about him.* Jesus needs us to bring peace to our world.*

SHARING

▶ How does Jesus need you?

▶ Jesus said the laborers were few. Are there too few persons spreading the Good News today? How could there be more?

▶ Share some stories of persons who have given their lives to the work of Jesus.

ACTION STEP

The two who have the same puzzle piece determine some action they can do to spread the kingdom of God, heal, or bring peace.

CLOSING PRAYER

Leader   Jesus, you sent your disciples in groups of two. Their companionship gave them strength and courage. They helped each other find the right words when teaching. They offered support in healing. They discovered ways to bring peace. Help us to do the same. Give us the unity to work together for the Kingdom. Give us the courage to speak about you. Send your Spirit upon us so that whatever we do points to you. We also ask that you bless missionaries who sacrifice their family and homeland to let others know about you. Send us forth now with a word from Scripture to help us to be missionaries to the people we will meet this week.

As persons leave, they select a Scripture verse from a box or basket.

OPTIONAL ACTIVITIES FOR FAMILY OR GROUPS

1. With a map or globe or headlines from a newspaper decide upon an area of the world to keep in prayer. Perhaps aid consciousness by eating an ethnic food from the country or learning something about the people.

2. Find out the names of missionaries from your diocese. E-mail them a supportive letter of thanks or make a contribution to their mission.

3. Invite a priest or sister for a meal. Let this person tell about the ministries they have in the Church and share your own ways to evangelize.

Not So Easy— Choosing God's Will

BEFORE YOU BEGIN

Materials: signs saying "Good" and "Evil"; props or signs indicating choices as given below in the Reflection.

To do: assign readers and persons to dramatize moral situations in Reflection

SONG

Theme of doing God's will, being a disciple, or making good choices

OPENING PRAYER

Leader   The response is "Holy Spirit, share your gift of understanding."
Father and Son, send us your Holy Spirit, we pray... (R)
Teach us to be true to our beliefs, we pray... (R)
Help us to choose the wisest course of action, we pray... (R)
Keep us from choosing evil, we pray... (R)
Strengthen our will to do good, we pray... (R)
Direct us in doing God's will, we pray... (R)
Center us on Jesus, we pray... (R)

READING: *Matthew 21:28–32*

Narrator	Jesus said to the chief priests and elders:
Jesus	What do you think? A man had two sons; he went to the first and said,
Father	Son, go and work in the vineyard today.
Son #1	I will not.
Jesus	But later he changed his mind and went. The father went to the second and said the same; and he answered,
Son #2	I go, sir.
Jesus	But he did not go. Which of the two did the will of his father?
People	The first.
Jesus	Truly I tell you, the tax collectors and the prostitutes are going into the kingdom of God ahead of you. For John came to you in the way of righteousness and you did not believe him, but the tax collectors and the prostitutes believed him; and even after you saw it, you did not change your minds and believe him.

REFLECTION

Dramatize a person choosing between good and evil and easily choosing good. Then the same person chooses between three sets of two good things: (a) cake and pie, (b) donating time or money to Habitat for Humanity, (c) joining a prayer group and spending more time with family.

Choosing between good and evil may sometimes be difficult, but often it is clear. We know what's wrong, and we either avoid it or do it. We know what's good and we either avoid it or do it. We obey our parents or disobey them, we cheat on a test or do our schoolwork honestly, or we give an honest day's work or slack off. Today's reading seems simple at first: one son says he will not obey but reconsiders and does his father's wishes. The other son claims to obey but never gets around to working in the vineyard. Which son is good? Is the first son good, because he gets the work done and the second son bad because he doesn't? On the surface level, the answer is obvious: Jesus is praising results. The one who does the Father's will is good.

What is not so clear is the motive of the heart. Why did the first son finally go to the vineyard? Was he motivated by fear of punishment, lack of money from a poor grape crop, or obedience to and love of his father? Why did the second son not go to the vineyard? Did he think he could get away with it? Was it only the thought that counted? Did another option occur that looked better than working in a vineyard? Was he going to get around to it?

In our own lives, we have experienced that choosing between two good things is harder than choosing between good and evil. Often the choice is between something good in my heart and the knowledge that what I am doing is the will of the Father. The difference between these two good things (the good in my heart and the will of God) is difficult to determine. I may, for example, feel in my heart that I should do something significant for the needy, or I may feel that I should confront someone with a problem, or I may feel I should change the style of my prayer or quit my job or leave a relationship. But what does God want? There's no compass to direct me. A friend or spiritual director or book may help, but it is my choice to determine whether the thing is my will or God's will. At such times we need to be deeply spiritual persons; that is, persons who put on the mind of God and "breathe" with the Spirit of God and become one with the God we seek.

SHARING

▶ When were you like the first son who said no, but eventually did what the father asked? When were you like the second son?

▶ What do you do when you feel like choosing something bad?

▶ What do you do when you need to decide between two good things to do?

▶ How do you know God's will for you?

▶ How can you know the mind of God and become one with God?

ACTION STEP

Do a good thing that you have been intending to do.

Do some study in an area like decision making, making moral choices, growing in the stages of moral or faith development (Lawrence Kohlberg, James Fowler, etc.), or doing the will of God.

Take time to listen to someone who has an important decision to make.

If you have to make a decision, write down all the pros and cons and weigh the alternatives. Or spend three days feeling the decision is X, then spend three days feeling the decision is Y. Which feels better? Which feels right? Which seems to be in keeping with God's plan for you?

CLOSING PRAYER

Leader   We thank you, O God, for the hard choices in our lives, because these times have strengthened our faith. Keep our eyes on you that we may always see what you would do. Keep our ears attuned to your voice, that we may know what you want us to do. Keep our hearts close to you that you may change us to become more and more like you. Grant us the ability to know and love you now and forever. Amen.

OPTIONAL ACTIVITIES FOR FAMILIES AND GROUPS

1. Use modeling clay to make a representation of God and yourself. Mold them together to show that closeness to God will help us do the will of God.

2. To an age-appropriate degree, discuss moral development, starting with babies who feel they are the center of the world and demonstrating that growth means widening our view of the world.

3. Discuss a family situation. What choices need to be made? Which choices reflect God's will?

4. Discuss examples from family life that parallel the responses of the two sons.

Surprise! A Party!

BEFORE YOU BEGIN

Materials: party decorations

To do: decorate the room for a party; select persons to dramatize reading

SONG

Theme of forgiveness

OPENING PRAYER

Leader   The response is "Forgive us, O God."

                When we do not live our baptismal promises, (R)

                When we do not follow the gospel, (R)

                When we let ourselves be led into temptation, (R)

                When we do not take care of the sick and needy, (R)

                When we do not obey, (R)

                When we say hurtful things, (R)

                When we steal or cheat, (R)

                When we do not take care of the earth, (R)

                When we do not pray, (R)

READING: *Luke 15:11–24 (This can be dramatized or pantomimed)*

Reader 1   There was a man who had two sons. The younger of them said to his father,

Son   Father, give me the share of the property that will belong to me.

Reader 2   So he divided his property between them. A few days later the younger son gathered all he had and traveled to a distant country, and there he squandered his property in dissolute living. When he had spent everything, a severe famine took place throughout that country, and he began to be in need.

Reader 3   So he went and hired himself out to one of the citizens of that country, who sent him to his fields to feed the pigs. He would gladly have filled himself with the pods that the pigs were eating; and no one gave him anything. But when he came to himself he said,

Son   How many of my father's hired hands have bread enough and to spare, but here I am dying of hunger! I will get up and go to my father, and I will say to him, "Father, I have sinned against heaven and before you; I am no longer worthy to be called your son; treat me like one of your hired hands."

Reader 4   So he set off and went to his father. But while he was still far off, his father saw him and was filled with compassion; he ran and put his arms around him and kissed him. Then the son said to him,

Son   Father, I have sinned against heaven and before you; I am no longer worthy to be called your son.

Reader 1   But the father said to his slaves,

Father   Quickly, bring out a robe—the best one—and put it on him; put a ring on his finger and sandals on his feet. And get the fatted calf and kill it, and let us eat and celebrate; for this son of mine was dead and is alive; he was lost and is found!

Reader 2   And they began to celebrate.

REFLECTION *(At the asterisk, yell "Surprise!")*

Jesus was a very good storyteller. He not only had a surprise ending, he had surprises all over this story, a parable. The younger son asked for his share of the inheritance.* In Jesus' day only the oldest received the inheritance. It would be quite a surprise for the younger son to get some inheritance. And the Father gave him the money!* Children, do you think your parents would give you your inheritance before they died? The boy became hungry and got a job feeding pigs.* No Jew would feed pigs. Pigs were considered unclean animals, animals that should never be raised, touched, or eaten. When the boy came home, the father gave him shoes and a robe.* Shoes and robes would not be worn by hired hands. They would be worn by members of the household, so the boy was back in the family. The son was given a ring.* A ring meant the boy could take care of finances. Would you allow this son to write checks after he wasted lots of money? The biggest surprise of all was the party with the fatted calf.* Jesus told us this story to show how completely God forgives us when we go away from him.

SHARING

▶ What do you like about this story? Do you find anything disturbing? Why?

▶ What is the point of this story? Why does Jesus use so many surprises?

▶ Share a time when you found it difficult to forgive.

▶ Even though we forgive, we do not forget. How do we know then that we have truly forgiven?

▶ The father in this story who does surprising things represents God. Do you find God surprising? Has God ever surprised you?

▶ Conclude the sharing with a small party. If someone in the group has recently received an honor or achieved something important, surprise that person with special recognition.

ACTION STEP

If you are in a situation requiring forgiveness, make the first move.

Learn how governments can forgive the debts owed them by other countries.

Take two minutes every day to examine your conscience. Simply ask yourself, "How have others seen Christ today through me?" If negative aspects of the day outweigh the positive, forgive yourself.

CLOSING PRAYER *(To be read by a child)*

Jesus, you told a story about God. I like the story, because the Father waited for his son to come home. The Father didn't make his son feel bad when he came home. He didn't say, "Where have you been?" He didn't punish him. Instead, he threw a party for him. The Father forgave everything. That's nice to know. God, you will always forgive me when I have been bad. Thank you, God, for understanding when I am not good. Help me to forgive others when they hurt me.

OPTIONAL ACTIVITIES FOR FAMILIES AND GROUPS

1. If family reconciliation is needed, prepare a ritual. For example, each family member has a real or silk flower. Each goes to other family members one at a time, expresses sorrow for hurt, and exchanges the flower. The flower represents the love that should be exchanged among the members. When flowers have been exchanged, each person may state one thing he or she intends to change; for example, "I will keep my room cleaner" or "I will try to be more patient."

2. The Ten Commandments are guidelines for leading a moral life. If family members need to memorize the Ten Commandments, conduct a game of putting them in numerical order.

3. Talk about the importance of forgiving oneself. Include how physical ailments may occasionally arise from a lack of forgiveness or deep-seated anger.

He Has Done Everything Well

BEFORE YOU BEGIN

Materials: a flashlight labeled "Christian" and batteries for Opening Prayer and Reflection

To do: assign readers

SONG

Theme of healing, praise of God, or season of the church year

OPENING PRAYER

Leader Jesus, born in Bethlehem over 2000 years ago, you will come again at the end of time. Now in the in-between time, help us continue your work.

All Jesus, we are proud of our name "Christian." We ask you to make us true to this name in all that we think, say, and do. Make your way of thinking our way. Make your actions ours. Make the love behind your words the love behind our words. Help us do everything well.

READING: *Mark 7:32–37*

Reader 1   The people brought to Jesus a deaf man who had an impediment in his speech; and they begged him to lay his hand on him. He took him aside in private, away from the crowd, and put his fingers into his ears, and he spat and touched his tongue.

Reader 2   Then looking up to heaven, he sighed and said, "Ephphatha," that is, "Be opened." And immediately his ears were opened, his tongue was released, and he spoke plainly.

Reader 3   Then Jesus ordered them to tell no one; but the more he ordered them, the more zealously they proclaimed it.

Reader 4   They were astounded beyond measure, saying, "He has done everything well; he even makes the deaf to hear and the mute to speak."

REFLECTION

Baptism gave us the name "Christian" and marked us as one of Christ's own. As followers, we must do as Christ did. We need to see with the eyes of Christ, hear with the ears of Christ, and think with the mind of Christ. In the account of Jesus with the deaf man we see Jesus' compassion and his healing power. With the crowd, we notice that Jesus has done everything well. Nothing is left unfinished; nothing is done haphazardly or without thought. All is done perfectly: Jesus is sensitive to the deaf man's need for privacy, Jesus calls upon his Father, and he uses signs that the deaf man can understand. The people saw that all was very good. Eons before, the Trinity in creation saw that all was very good; however, human beings spoiled God's plan for creation. Now Jesus is restoring the plan by doing everything well. We can help Jesus; we can extend the work of his plan. But we need to stay connected to him; we need to be interlocked with him. Our motto must be "With Christ, in Christ, and through Christ."

SHARING

▶ Saint Paul often used phrases like *with Christ*, *in Christ*, and *through Christ*. Paul uses these terms to show we are in close relationship with Christ. Actually, we are being made into his likeness. How do you put on the mind of Christ? How do you model your life on that of Christ? How do you stay connected with Christ?

▶ Healing is a gift of the Holy Spirit, enabling us to imitate Christ when he healed. How have you used your baptismal gift of healing? How have you experienced healing through the prayer of others?

▶ How can you imitate Jesus' sensitivity that would never embarrass anyone?

▶ How are you continuing the plan of creation to keep all things good? How are you doing "everything well"?

▶ Do your words show gratitude for the gift of speech and hearing?

ACTION STEP

Read inspirational stories, a spiritual classic, or information on social justice.

Include in your conversation this week comments about how you have noticed that persons connected to Jesus Christ do his work.

"Re-connect" with Jesus this week through extra prayer. Perhaps consider making a retreat.

CLOSING PRAYER

Leader   Please stand in a circle. Take turns stating something for which you are grateful, something that is usually taken for granted, such as the gift of speaking. After each, we will all respond, "Thank you, God."

Examples: "For the gift of listening, thank you, God" or "For the gift of instantaneous communication, thank you, God."

OPTIONAL ACTIVITIES FOR FAMILIES AND GROUPS

1. On a paper write "We have done these things well." When a family member has done something well, add it to the list. At the end of the week celebrate these good things with a special commendation or treat.

2. Put two interlocking paper clips in your pocket. When you feel them, remind yourself that you are linked to Christ and help him do the work of creation.

3. Discuss ways to become more sensitive and respectful to persons who have disabilities or different abilities.

Interdependence

BEFORE YOU BEGIN

Materials: dot-to-dot pictures or puzzles—one for each group

To do: assign readers

SONG

Theme of praying or working together

OPENING PRAYER

Leader   The response is "God of connections, hear our prayer."

Gracious Father, bless our families with unity. (R)

Life-giving Creator, guide us to see our universe as interdependent. (R)

Jesus our Brother, connect all human beings in brotherhood and sisterhood. (R)

Jesus our Friend, give us openness to making new friends. (R)

Spirit of Love, be the bond among the members of our church. (R)

Spirit of Compassion, help us know when to get involved in the lives of others. (R)

READING: *Matthew 18:15–20*

Reader 1   If another member of the church sins against you, go and point out the fault when the two of you are alone. If the member listens to you, you have regained that one.

Reader 2   But if you are not listened to, take one or two others along with you, so that every word may be confirmed by the evidence of two or three witnesses.

Reader 3   If the member refuses to listen to them, tell it to the church; and if the offender refuses to listen even to the church, let such a one be to you as a Gentile and a tax collector.

Reader 4   Truly I tell you, whatever you bind on earth will be bound in heaven, and whatever you loose on earth will be loosed in heaven.

Reader 5   Again, truly I tell you, if two of you agree on earth about anything you ask, it will be done for you by my Father in heaven. For where two or three are gathered in my name, I am there among them.

REFLECTION

Teams of intergenerational participants race to finish a dot-to-dot picture, put a small puzzle together, or do some other short activity that requires connecting things.

Your activity required two things: connecting things and being connected yourselves. You depended upon each other to make the right move, or you depended upon someone to stay out of the way while you made the right move. Because your group included children, teens, and adults, it was an intergenerational activity. Because you depended upon each other, it was also an interdependent activity.

Today's reading shows interdependence. When a church member sinned but wasn't aware that the sin was hurting others, one or more other church members went to talk to the person. That's what our church community should do: have the courage to help one another when things are not right. We should support people when they are in trouble or need. In addition, there are many other ways to be interdependent as a church community; for example, we can drive those who do not drive, we can use our talents to repair a car or computer, we can ask for help when there's a mailing to do, or we can all take turns working at a church festival.

Another way to be interdependent is in our prayer. Jesus said that wherever two or three are gathered, he is there. When our families gather for food, fun, work, or prayer, Jesus is there. When our church gathers, Jesus is there. When small groups gather, Jesus is there. Our prayer is interdependent; that is, we add to the effectiveness of our prayer when others pray with us. And, of course, we depend upon God to hear our prayer, so our prayer is interdependent with God. And God depends on us, too, to pray and work to bring about the reign of God.

SHARING

▶ Discuss times when your family or your church community was interdependent. How did that feel? What was the result?

▶ Have you ever prayed with others for a common intention; for example, did a group pray for someone's healing? What happened?

▶ If someone is doing wrong and you feel you need to be involved to correct the wrong, what are the steps to take to correct the wrong with love?

ACTION STEP

Form prayer groups to meet to pray for common concerns.

Study ways to correct wrongdoing effectively and lovingly.

Study the interconnectedness of all creation. Note how we are all made from stardust. Love creation and take steps to care for all God's creatures.

CLOSING PRAYER

Leader   Jesus said that wherever two or three are gathered in his name, he is there in their midst. For our prayer, let us lift up the names of groups that do the work of God. Whenever a group is mentioned, we will respond, "Teach them to pray well." Examples could include social justice groups, churches, Christian musicians, your own families and prayer groups, and so on.

OPTIONAL ACTIVITIES FOR FAMILIES OR GROUPS

1. Write appreciation notes to those in your intergenerational group expressing how they have helped you or what the group sharing means to you.

2. As a family or group, decide to pray for a specific intention together and pray as a group as well as individually.

3. Discuss any unhealthy ways of being dependent; discuss how to replace these actions with those that are more interdependent.

What Are You Discussing along the Way?

BEFORE YOU BEGIN

Materials: floor markers, treats (for example, candy, cupcakes), music

To do: assign readers; arrange markers on the floor

SONG

Theme of servanthood

OPENING PRAYER

Leader   The response is "Help us to serve."
                   When we feel we are more important than others, (R)
                   When we want to show off, (R)
                   When we do not want to give up our time, (R)
                   When we are stingy with our talents and gifts, (R)
                   When we realize that what we do to others we do to Christ, (R)
                   When we remember that we are part of the reign of God, (R)

READING: *Mark 9:33–37*

Narrator   Then Jesus and his disciples came to Capernaum; and when he was in the house he asked them,

Jesus   What were you arguing about on the way?

Narrator   But they were silent, for on the way they had argued with one another who was the greatest. He sat down, called the twelve, and said to them,

Jesus   Whoever wants to be first must be last of all and servant of all.

Narrator   Then he took a little child and put it among them; and taking it in his arms, he said to them,

Jesus   Whoever welcomes one such child in my name welcomes me, and whoever welcomes me welcomes not me but the one who sent me.

REFLECTION

Before I begin the reflection, we will have an activity called a Candy Walk. There are about thirty papers on the floor. When the music stops, put your foot on a paper. Not everyone will have a paper, and those persons without a paper will be eliminated. Some papers will also be taken away. Eventually there will be only twelve papers on the floor, and the final twelve persons standing on a paper will receive candy.

> *The game is played before the leader continues the reflection. Note: Rules, numbers, and type of treat may be altered to fit the group. After the game, the leader continues with the following:]*

As you enjoyed the walk, what were you talking about? The conversation probably centered on wanting a treat, getting on a paper first, and wondering whether the treats would run out. We were somewhat like the disciples as they went to Capernaum. They were arguing about who was the greatest. Jesus answered their argument by saying the first must be last, the greatest must be the least, and the most powerful must be a servant. In other words, Jesus would say the greatest are those who received the last treat and those who let others win to make sure others got a treat before them.

The reign of God is the opposite of kingdoms on earth. Here the powerful persons have money, the people with the most votes win elections, the governments with a lot of weapons rule over countries with few weapons. The reign of God is for the least, the powerless, the poor, and for all the powerful and wealthy who are servants. The reign of God is for anyone who treats others with the dignity they deserve. The reign of God is for those who are like servants, looking out for the welfare of others and taking care of their needs. The reign of God is for those who are like children, those who trust God their good Parent and realize that they depend upon others.

SHARING

▶ What is it like to be a servant? Why did Jesus use a "servant" as a model for those who would become citizens of heaven?

▶ What is it like to be a child? Why did Jesus use the image of child to talk about the reign of God?

▶ Share a time when you put others before your own convenience. How did that feel? What was the result?

▶ What steps do you take after an argument to repair the damage? Is the damage ever completely healed?

ACTION STEP

Look at the ordinary things you do during the week. Consider how you can bring the attitude of a servant to your home, school, place of employment, and recreation spots.

Learn how to "argue" more effectively in a Christian manner.

Take an action step on behalf of the poor and needy. Check the church bulletin for such opportunities.

CLOSING PRAYER

Leader   The response is "Talk to us along the way."
Jesus, you talked to the elders in the Temple, teaching them from your wisdom. (R)
Jesus, you talked to your disciples as you walked the roads of the Holy Land. (R)
Jesus, you talked to the Samaritan woman when no one else spoke to her. (R)
Jesus, you talked to lepers when everyone else avoided them. (R)
Jesus, you talked to the crowds and healed the sick, even when you wanted to be alone. (R)
Jesus, you talked words of compassion to many on the day of your death. (R)
Jesus, you talked with your disciples before your Ascension, saying, "These are my words that I spoke to you while I was still with you—that everything written about me in the law of Moses, the prophets, and the psalms must be fulfilled." (R)
Jesus, you talked to the couple on the road to Emmaus and their hearts burned within them. (R)
Jesus, be with us in everything we do this week. (R)

OPTIONAL ACTIVITIES FOR FAMILIES OR GROUPS

1. Talk about things that are upside down. Jesus sometimes asks us to be "upside down" that is, do things in a way opposite the message of media or advertisements. When watching commercials, point out what Jesus might say.

2. As a family, practice being servants together by doing yard work or housework for yourselves or others. Instead of a Job Jar or To Do list, have a Servant Jar or Servant List.

Who Do You Say that I Am?

BEFORE YOU BEGIN

Materials: papers with "Who do you say that I am?" written at top for everyone; one pencil or watercolor marker for everyone

To do: assign readers

SONG

Theme about Jesus as Messiah or a song of praise

OPENING PRAYER *(At the asterisk, all say "So much more!")*

We come before you, O God, with a question: "Who are you?" So often we think we know, but you are so much more.* We have a picture of you in mind. We think of you as Father or Friend or Savior or the Big Man in the Sky. But you are so much more.* We think we know you, because we have gone to religion classes, but you are so much more.* We think we know you, because we read the Bible or listen to homilies, but you are so much more.* Help us realize that we can never begin to fully understand you, because you are so much more.* O God, we believe that you are so much more.*

READING: *Mark 8:27–35*

Narrator   Jesus went on with his disciples to the villages of Caesarea Philippi; and on the way he asked his disciples,

Jesus   Who do people say that I am?

Narrator   And they answered him,

Disciple 1   John the Baptist

Disciple 2   And others, Elijah;

Disciple 3   And still others, one of the prophets.

Narrator   He asked them,

Jesus   But who do you say that I am?

Narrator   Peter answered him,

Peter   You are the Messiah.

Narrator   And he sternly ordered them not to tell anyone about him.

REFLECTION

Pin or tape "Who do you say that I am?" papers on each person's back.

On your back you have a paper asking an important question, the same question Jesus asked: "Who do you say that I am?" For several minutes go from one person to the next and let each write a word or phrase about you, and you do the same in return. Examples might include nouns like *friend, son, niece, teacher, student, attorney* or *grandmother*; or descriptive words like *caring, trustworthy, reliable, industrious, fun-loving*. Of course, these should be all positive things.

After this activity, allow a few minutes for persons to read the responses.

God knows everything, but Jesus in his human nature had to learn and discover. Jesus needed to keep discovering his identity, even as we do. Teens wonder, "Who am I? What role do I have to play on this earth?" People facing retirement ask similar questions: "Who am I when I no longer have a job?" Jesus and we want to know what other persons are thinking of us. Jesus perhaps wondered, "Are my disciples ready to follow me to the cross? Do the people of Israel realize I am the Messiah? Is the time ripe for me to fully reveal the plan of salvation?" So Jesus asked and received the half-certain, half-uncertain answer: You are the Messiah. Jesus then knew that the time was approaching to lose his life in the act of establishing the reign of God on earth.

SHARING

▶   Did you discover anything about yourself or someone else when comparing the papers on your back? Could God be telling you something through these responses? Do these responses indicate how you can help bring about the reign of God on earth?

▶ Share a time when you were uncertain about who you were. How was this uncertainty resolved?

▶ Who do you say Jesus is? Do you have a special name for Jesus? Which scriptural title of Jesus do you prefer, such as Good Shepherd, Savior, King, Truth, Life, and so on? In what way do you address God, the Trinity?

▶ How do you think Jesus felt about the responses John the Baptist, Elijah, one of the prophets, and the Messiah?

▶ Has there been a "point of no return" in your life? Was there some leap into the future with no looking back? How did you make that leap? Did your faith help you on this occasion?

ACTION STEP

Take some quiet time to discover yourself. Perhaps spend a quiet hour in a park, a silent hour at home in your room, or make a longer retreat.

Read articles or books on human development or aging or self-actualization.

Study the theology of Jesus' knowledge as a human.

Listen to someone who is growing in self-knowledge, perhaps someone wondering what the next move in life will be.

CLOSING PRAYER

Leader   During our closing prayer a small group will softly repeat "Who do you say that I am?" like an ostinato. Whenever you feel moved to do so, call out a name for God. We will all silently adore God under that title until the next name is called. Leave about five seconds between names.

OPTIONAL ACTIVITIES FOR FAMILIES AND GROUPS

1. Page through one of the Gospels. Whenever you find an answer to the question "Who is Jesus?" draw a picture on a scroll of paper.

2. Write the alphabet. Beside each letter write a word or phrase that describes God, for example, *awesome, bountiful giver, caring, divine.*

3. Pull crayons from a box of crayons and compare God to that color; for example, "God is like a white crayon, because God contains everything, all colors" or "God is like green, because green is everywhere" or "God is like gold, because God is precious and valuable."

Multiplication of the Loaves and Fish

BEFORE YOU BEGIN

Materials: symbols of Eucharist, such as bread, wine (water with red food coloring), wheat sheaf, grapes (optional)

To do: assign readers

SONG

Song with theme about Eucharist, thanksgiving, or sharing

OPENING PRAYER

Leader	You, O Lord, are the Bread of Life.
All	May we always eat of this bread and become what we eat.
Leader	We thank you, Bread of Life, for feeding us.
All	May we always eat of this bread and become what we eat.
Leader	We thank you, Bread of Life, for sharing yourself with us.
All	May we share ourselves with others.

READING: *John 6:2–15*

Narrator	A large crowd kept following [Jesus], because they saw the signs that he was doing for the sick. Jesus went up the mountain and sat down there with his disciples. Now the Passover, the festival of the Jews, was near. When he looked up and saw a large crowd coming toward him, Jesus said to Philip,
Jesus	Where are we to buy bread for these people to eat?"
Narrator	He said this to test him, for he himself knew what he was going to do. Philip answered him,
Philip	Six months' wages would not buy enough bread for each of them to get a little.
Narrator	One of his disciples, Andrew, Simon Peter's brother, said to him,
Andrew	There is a boy here who has five barley loaves and two fish. But what are they among so many people?
Jesus	Make the people sit down.
Narrator	Now there was a great deal of grass in the place; so they sat down, about five thousand in all. Then Jesus took the loaves, and when he had given thanks, he distributed them to those who were seated; so also the fish, as much as they wanted. When they were satisfied, he told his disciples,
Jesus	Gather up the fragments left over, so that nothing may be lost.
Narrator	So they gathered them up, and from the fragments of the five barley loaves, left by those who had eaten, they filled twelve baskets. When the people saw the sign that he had done, they began to say,
People	This is indeed the prophet who is to come into the world.
Narrator	When Jesus realized that they were about to come and take him by force to make him king, he withdrew again to the mountain by himself.

REFLECTION

As the leader reads the reflection, participants can gesture the actions of taking, thanking, breaking and giving at the asterisk.

Whenever we read a story in Scripture containing the words* *take, thank, break,* and *give,* we know we should think of Eucharist. Often in the Gospels Jesus is at a meal.* Sometimes Jesus provides the meal. Remember the time he prepared a breakfast on the shore for his apostles?* Sometimes he was invited to the meal. Do you remember when Jesus invited himself to dine at Zacchaeus' house?* Sometimes he simply enjoyed the meal. Do you remember how he went to the home of Martha and Mary? Perhaps Jesus was just relaxing and enjoying some good home cooking.* Jesus did many things at a meal besides eat food. Sometimes Jesus taught about the Kingdom, sometimes he sent people on mission, sometimes he forgave and redeemed.* The most important meal of all was the Last Supper. The Last Supper linked Jesus' life and mission to his death-resurrection.* If we look at all the meals, we see so often that thanksgiving and sharing go together. Think of the meals you eat. Are you thankful? Do you share? Think of the times you go to Eucharist. Are you thankful? After Mass, do you share what you hear? Do you live like Christ whom you received in Eucharist?*

SHARING

▶ Is there a word or phrase from this story that struck you?

▶ As soon as Jesus saw the crowd, he wanted to offer hospitality. Do you recall other occasions when Jesus offered hospitality? As followers of Jesus, how can we offer hospitality?

▶ Andrew and the little boy offered all they had—just five barley loaves and two fish. Jesus transformed the meager food into a plentiful meal. Share a time when God took the little you offered and used it for something much bigger.

▶ Jesus asked his disciples to gather the leftovers so that nothing would be wasted. Do you use all the gifts God has given you?

▶ The people wanted Jesus to become their king. Perhaps this was a temptation for Jesus like the one he experienced in the desert when the devil tempted him to make bread from stones. Perhaps once again Jesus had to say, "One does not live by bread alone, but by every word that comes from the mouth of God" (Mt. 3:4). What in your life is "bread" that you want in abundance? Is there something more important than this "bread"?

▶ Jesus thanked his Father and then shared the loaves and fish. Share a time when your gratitude led you to share.

ACTION STEP

Share your time, talent, or treasure with someone less fortunate.

If possible, spend extra time praying before a tabernacle.

CLOSING PRAYER

Leader	Bread of Life, when you ate in the house of Levi, you healed sinners.
All	Through your gift of Eucharist, heal us.
Leader	Bread of Life, when you nourished the crowd, you thanked and shared.
All	Through your gift of Eucharist, help us be more thankful and generous.
Leader	Bread of Life, when you dined with Mary and Martha, you reminded these two sisters of the importance of listening to you.
All	Through your gift of Eucharist, help us to listen to your Word and live it.
Leader	Bread of Life, when you ate with a leading Pharisee, you taught us to include everyone.
All	Through your gift of Eucharist, unite our world as brothers and sisters.

Leader   Bread of Life, at the Last Supper, you gave yourself as food.

All   Through the gift of Eucharist, make us more willing to feed others in their hunger for food, love, and all other needs.

OPTIONAL ACTIVITIES FOR FAMILIES OR GROUPS

1. Make a poster of those persons and things for which you are grateful.

2. Plan an action that will alleviate world hunger.

3. Dramatize the story of the multiplication of the loaves and fish.

4. Compare the story of the multiplication of the loaves and fish with the story of Emmaus (Luke 24:13–35). Look for the words *take, thank, break,* and *give.*

Petition in Jesus' Name

BEFORE YOU BEGIN

Materials: Bible, candle, a paper or scroll on which is written "Petition in Jesus' Name"

To do: assign readers and children to dramatize

SONG

Theme of prayer, Holy Spirit, or praise

OPENING PRAYER

Leader	Holy Spirit, help us to pray.
All	Holy Spirit, pray in us.
Leader	Holy Spirit, you speak our petitions.
All	Holy Spirit, pray in us.
Leader	Holy Spirit, you are our answer to prayer.
All	Holy Spirit, pray in us.

READING: *John 16:23–27*

Narrator Jesus said:

Jesus Very truly, I tell you, if you ask anything of the Father in my name, he will give it to you. Until now you have not asked for anything in my name. Ask and you will receive, so that your joy may be complete. I have said these things to you in figures of speech. The hour is coming when I will no longer speak to you in figures, but will tell you plainly of the Father. On that day you will ask in my name. I do not say to you that I will ask the Father on your behalf; for the Father himself loves you, because you have loved me and have believed that I came from God.

REFLECTION

Today we will talk about asking God for the things we need. First, we have a couple of skits prepared by the children.

> *Skits: Children dramatize pleading with their parents, grandparents, or sitters to receive something, such as a toy, ice cream, permission to visit a friend or go to a movie*

When children ask for things, they add clout by bringing in someone else's name: "Daddy said I could" and "Grandma would let me" and "My teacher would like it." Jesus tells his disciples and us that effective prayer is done in his name. The next time you pray, add clout to your prayer; for example, "Father, in the name of Jesus your son, I ask healing for…" or "In the name of Jesus Christ I beg blessing upon…."

If we do not pray in Jesus' name, does that mean our prayer is not heard? No, there is also the implicit, silent use of Jesus' name, when we live our whole lives in Jesus. We have desires and needs all day long, we are hungry for better things all the time, and in a sense we ourselves become a petition. God is so present and attentive to us that God is attentive to the jumbled desires of our hearts. At those times praying in Jesus' name means entering into Jesus, living in him. Moreover, the Spirit prays in us. We can unite ourselves to the prayer of the Spirit which is always done through Jesus. We could begin our day with this simple prayer: "Holy Spirit, pray in me. Let all my little prayers be caught up in your one great prayer. I trust that my prayer will be answered, because you, O God, are always with me. What more could I want? Help me be attentive to the many blessings you will give me today."

SHARING

- ▶ Describe the way you pray. Has your style of praying changed over the years?
- ▶ To whom do you pray? Do you think of the Trinity or individual persons in the Trinity? Do you pray through the intercession of a saint?
- ▶ How do you respond to someone who says "I prayed, but God didn't answer me"?
- ▶ We speak of different types of prayer: petition, thanksgiving, adoration, contrition. Is one better than the other? Do you include all these types?
- ▶ What is your favorite prayer?

ACTION STEP

Consider joining or starting a prayer group, perhaps a weekly gathering for intercessory prayer or songs of worship or Scripture reading.

Consider experimenting with a different style of prayer, such as meditation, the Jesus Prayer, the rosary.

Locate a good website for daily prayer and meditation, put it under "Favorites," and use it frequently.

FINAL PRAYER

Leader   Let us pray the prayer Jesus taught us and be very attentive to its meaning.

All   Our Father...

OPTIONAL ACTIVITIES FOR FAMILIES AND GROUPS

1. Listen to a worship song and make up a dance to it.

2. Gather some neighbors to pray for a specific need. Perhaps go to the home of someone who is ill to pray for that person.

3. Use a magazine or newspaper for family or group prayer by turning the pages, occasionally stopping to pray when illustrations suggest needs, such as government leaders, victims of natural disasters, and those who have recently died.

The Lord Was Moved with Pity

BEFORE YOU BEGIN

Materials: Bible and candles, box and cards with instruction for pantomiming the Reflection

To do: assign readers and persons to dramatize

SONG

Theme of healing, comfort

OPENING PRAYER

Leader	Jesus, you are so much a part of us, so close to us.
All	We can tell you anything, and you will understand.
Leader	Jesus, you carry us over the rough spots.
All	When things go wrong, we can go to you for comfort.
Leader	Jesus, you are a brother to us, a "God-Brother."
All	Make us one family with you and all our brothers and sisters around the world.

READING: *Luke 7:11–17*

Narrator Jesus went to a town called Nain, and his disciples and a large crowd went with him. As he approached the gate of the town, a man who had died was being carried out. He was his mother's only son, and she was a widow; and with her was a large crowd from the town. When the Lord saw her, he had compassion for her and said to her,

Jesus Do not weep.

Narrator 2 Then he came forward and touched the bier, and the bearers stood still. And he said,

Jesus Young man, I say to you, rise!

Narrator 3 The dead man sat up and began to speak, and Jesus gave him to his mother. Fear seized all of them, and they glorified God, saying,

People A great prophet has risen among us! God has looked favorably on his people!

REFLECTION

Jesus was one of us, completely human, completely involved in our world, feeling all the things we feel. In the box are phrases that the volunteers in groups of two will pantomime. We will guess what they are doing, and then we will apply the phrase to Jesus.

> *The cards drawn from the box have the words in bold print. After each is pantomimed, the leader adds the application to Jesus.*

(A) GIVE A HUG. Jesus loved tenderly. He was there for people in their pain.

(B) PICK A FLOWER AND SMELL IT. Jesus loved the earth, the flowers, all creatures.

(C) HELP SOMEONE WHO FALLS DOWN. Jesus helped those who were injured: the lame, the deaf, those possessed by evil spirits.

(D) COMFORT SOMEONE WHO IS IN PAIN. Jesus was a healer, who did not want people to suffer. He cured them of their bent backs, their paralysis, their bleeding, their leprosy.

(E) BE COMPASSIONATE TOWARD SOMEONE WHO IS CRYING. Jesus felt sorry for those who were in sorrow, those in tears. He helped these persons by feeling their pain, too, and by giving the people reason to rejoice.

SHARING

▶ Why do you think Jesus raised the young man from the dead?

▶ In the original language of the gospels, the word "compassion" suggests that Jesus was moved very deeply with the greatest sympathy and empathy. Does your image of God include God's compassion and empathy? When have you experienced God's compassion?

▶ Share a time when you were able to relieve someone of great sorrow. How can one express sympathy best?

ACTION STEP

Be life-giving through your optimism and positive outlook.

Take more interest in social justice issues.

CLOSING PRAYER

Leader   Let us pray for a heart like the heart of Jesus, full of compassion.

All   O God of Goodness and Compassion, you are always attentive to us in our every need. Expand our hearts with your love to include everyone in need of our care. Help us to serve you in our brothers and sisters, especially those who are in sorrow. Help us comfort the poor, sick, and suffering. Hear our prayer, for you are a God of mercy.

Transfiguration

BEFORE YOU BEGIN

Materials: (optional) Bible and candle

To do: assign readers; two persons practice the Reflection one representing Jesus and one working the spotlight

SONG

Song about Transfiguration, prayer, or season of the church year

OPENING PRAYER

Leader	God of Light, let us see your glory.
All	O God, show us your face.
Leader	God of Power, let us see your mighty deeds.
All	O God, show us your face.
Leader	God of Transforming Love, make us loving.
All	O God, show us your face.

| Leader | God who hears our prayer, be near us when we pray. |
| All | O God, show us your face. |

READING: *Matthew 17:1–8*

Narrator 1	Jesus took with him Peter and James and his brother John and led them up a high mountain, by themselves.
Narrator 2	And he was transfigured before them, and his face shone like the sun, and his clothes became dazzling white. Suddenly there appeared to them Moses and Elijah, talking with him. Then Peter said to Jesus.
Peter	Lord, it is good for us to be here; if you wish, I will make three dwellings here, one for you, one for Moses, and one for Elijah.
Narrator 3	While he was still speaking, suddenly a bright cloud overshadowed them, and from the cloud a voice said,
Voice	This is my Son, the Beloved; with him I am well pleased; listen to him!
Narrator 4	When the disciples heard this, they fell to the ground and were overcome by fear. But Jesus came and touched them, saying
Jesus	Get up and do not be afraid.
Narrator 5	And when they looked up, they saw no one except Jesus himself alone.

REFLECTION

A person representing Jesus walks slowly in front of the group. At the asterisk, this person stops to pantomime or "become a statue" depicting what the leader says about the life of Jesus. When he is transfigured, a spotlight could be shone on him.

Jesus had been teaching and preaching* throughout his public life. He had worked many miracles like letting the lame and crippled walk.* He shared many meals.* The time was drawing near when Jesus realized that he would be put to death. One day Jesus decided to ask* his three best friends, Peter, James and John to go up a mountain* with him. On the mountain Jesus prayed* to his Father. As Jesus prayed, the radiant, brilliant light and life of God shone around him and in him. God the Father, God the Son in his human nature, and God the Holy Spirit were in deep conversation. The three disciples were amazed. Perhaps the disciples were beginning to learn the power of God that turns dying into victory. Perhaps the disciples would remember this day when they saw their Master put to death.

SHARING

▶ The fourth Luminous Mystery is the Transfiguration. Why do you feel the pope added this mystery to the rosary?

▶ What do you find most interesting in this story?

- What do you think the human prayer of Jesus was like when he prayed to his Father?
- How do you pray? Do you ever feel "transfigured" when you pray?

ACTION STEP

What needs to be transfigured in your home, school, or parish? Decide upon an action step to achieve the needed change.

What political, social, or economic issue in your area needs to be addressed? Decide upon an action step to address the issue.

CLOSING PRAYER

Leader   Jesus prayed to his Father. Let us reflect what this meant for Jesus to call God Father and for us to call God Father. I will say the word "Father" a few times, then you can say the word "Father" silently like a mantra (repeated prayer-word). We will be silent with the word "Father" for about three minutes until I begin the Our Father, when you can join me aloud.

OPTIONAL ACTIVITIES FOR FAMILIES OR GROUPS

1. Draw a picture of Jesus being transfigured on the mountain with his three disciples.

2. Dramatize the story of the Transfiguration.

3. Call a family meeting to discuss a family concern. When the concern is resolved, celebrate with a special treat.

Being Attracted to God

BEFORE YOU BEGIN

Materials: magnets and pictures of Jesus

To do: assign readers and actors

SONG

Song about discipleship

OPENING PRAYER

Leader	O God of Loveliness, we are attracted to you.
All	Draw us to you.
Leader	Jesus, we want to follow you more closely.
All	Draw us to you.
Leader	Jesus, when we would rather turn away from you.
All	Draw us to you.

READING: *Mark 16–20*

This reading could be dramatized, using a cast of six (omitting the hired men): Jesus, Simon, Andrew, James, John, and Zebedee.

Narrator   As Jesus passed along the Sea of Galilee, he saw Simon and his brother Andrew casting a net into the sea—for they were fisherman. And Jesus said to them,

Jesus   Follow me and I will make you fish for people.

Narrator   And immediately they left their nets and followed him. As he went a little farther, he saw James, son of Zebedee and his brother John, who were in their boat mending the nets. Immediately he called them; and they left their father Zebedee in the boat with the hired men, and followed him.

REFLECTION

Participants use magnets to pick up a picture of Jesus. If the pictures are different, participants should choose one that attracts them.

You have selected a picture of Jesus that attracted you. You selected it because you were drawn to it like a magnet. Why? What attracted you? What do you find attractive about prayer, worship, Scripture reading, good deeds, and, in a word, leading a spiritual life? On the other hand, is leading a spiritual life ever unattractive or distasteful? Would you rather do something else than pray or attend Mass? These feelings are not bad; even saints like Mother Teresa of Calcutta and Teresa of Avila didn't feel like praying for years at a time, but they kept their times of prayer faithfully. We will reflect upon the apostles when they were first attracted to Jesus. But we know that throughout the years they followed Jesus, it was not always so attractive. At times they thought of leaving Jesus, and some did. Even many of those who followed him during his entire public life abandoned him in the end at the time of his crucifixion.

SHARING

▶   What attracted Jesus to Simon, Andrew, James, and John? What attracted them to Jesus?

▶   Have you ever thought about leaving Jesus or not living your faith? What has helped you stay close to Jesus and to his Church?

▶   How do you "fish for people"? What in you helps attract persons to follow Jesus and live their faith? How do you support persons who attend to their spiritual lives?

▶   Share a time when you felt called by Jesus.

▶   How do you pray when prayer is easy? How do you pray when prayer is difficult?

ACTION STEP

Plan something you can do this week to follow Jesus more closely, such as extra prayer, acts of kindness, or reading Christian literature.

Speak to someone who is having difficulty following Jesus and living the faith.

Read the life of a saint who did not always follow the Lord.

CLOSING PRAYER

Leader Look at your picture of Christ as we pray.

Jesus Christ, you draw us to yourself in so many ways: the desires of our heart, the beauty of creation, the kindness of a friend, the sacraments, the words of Scripture, and all the events of our day. Help us be open to your call, listening for you with attentive reverence. When we hear your voice, help us to follow. Lead us in our oneness with you and the Holy Spirit, now and forever. Amen.

OPTIONAL ACTIVITIES FOR FAMILIES AND GROUPS

1. Draw a picture of Jesus calling his disciples. Draw a second picture of Jesus calling you.

2. Make a list of characteristics that draw us to Jesus. Then make a list of characteristics of persons in your family or group that are attractive. Where are the similarities?